PUB WALKS
from
COUNTRY STATIONS

Volume 2

(BUCKINGHAMSHIRE and OXFORDSHIRE)

Clive Higgs

The
Book
Castle

First published May 1998
by
The Book Castle
12 Church Street
Dunstable
Bedfordshire LU5 4RU

ISBN 1 871199 73 5

Computer typeset by Keyword, Aldbury, Hertfordshire.
Printed by Anthony Rowe Ltd., Chippenham, Wiltshire.

Cover photograph: Ellesborough Village from Coombe Hill
© Vaughan Basham

CONTENTS

THE AUTHOR

Clive Higgs was born in 1922 in the parish of Mortlake with East Sheen on the extremities of South West London. By 1930 his father had become an avid motorist. Summer Sundays featured the bonus of trips by car to the countryside of South East England, included with which were lavish picnics. Clive soon learned to read maps and became navigator on excursions to places such as The Meon Valley (Hampshire), Christmas Common (on The Chiltern Escarpment in Oxfordshire), Inkpen Beacon (where Berkshire, Hampshire and Wiltshire meet), etc., etc.

Unfortunately for the author the summer of 1935 saw his father's interest in the motor car replaced by the bowling green. Something had to be done to obviate Sundays spent in suburbia. With 2/6d (12½p) in his pocket, donated by his parents, he set off on his first ramble . . . from Boxhill railway station and up into the Surrey Downs at Ranmore Common. Clive has been an ardent rambler ever since, the only interruption being at the time when he served his country in the latter half of World War 2.

He also became a keen cyclist. At no time did the motor car hold any attraction for Clive Higgs, although oddly enough his entire professional career was devoted to the intricacies of vehicle insurance! His extensive knowledge of the highways and byways of South East England are unsurpassed. Even today at the age of 75, Clive regularly goes rambling and with the support of his wife, Anne, hopes to continue to do so for many years to come.

PROLOGUE TO BUCKINGHAMSHIRE

From the northern tip of the county some ten miles from Northampton town to the Berkshire border just above Slough is a distance of more than fifty miles. Hence Bucks can be said to be a link between London's suburbia and the pastures of the East Midlands. It is also bounded by Oxfordshire, Berkshire, Hertfordshire, Bedfordshire and Middlesex, the latter officially non-existent nowadays, being deemed by those who purport to know better to be part of Greater London.

The little rivers in the south of Bucks disport their contents into the mighty Thames, including Wycombe's Wye, and the Colne, the latter emanating from Hertfordshire. To the north of the county one encounters streams that flow northward to reach the sea via The Wash between the counties of Norfolk and Lincolnshire. Apart from the River Thame with its tiny tributaries which enters the Thames in Oxfordshire, the ridges of the Chiltern Hills form a watershed between those streams which flow south and those which flow north-eastwards.

The Chilterns form one of the major features of Bucks. The area is renowned for beech woods which form the wherewithal of the furniture industry around High Wycombe. The summits with extensive views over Aylesbury Vale are sometimes more than eight hundred feet in hight. Included in Bucks are Halton Hill and Coombe Hill (above Wendover), Parslows Hillock and Wain Hill (overlooking Princes Risborough). To the north-east and the south-west of these heights the Chiltern edge is in Bedfordshire and Oxfordshire respectively. The hinterland of these high places stretches some twenty miles south-east and contain a collection of villages and country lanes stretching almost to the very gateway of London's suburbia. Some of the most attractive parts of 'comuterland' fall within south-east Bucks.

North of the Chilterns, much of the county consists of the vast Vale of Aylesbury. Beef for the Royal Family's table used to be provided from this area in medieval times. The vale may look flat when viewed from nearby high places, but it is by no means so. There are abundant undulations and ridges of hills within, for example those upon which the villages of Brill and Quainton stand. Further to the north one encounters the vast conurbation around present day Milton Keynes. Many a rural walk has been obliterated by this example of 'progress'.

The county is well served by railways. London Underground's Metropolitan Line penetrates as far as Amersham. Chiltern Railways operate from Marylebone through Amersham *en route* to the county town of Aylesbury. A second 'arm' of the same line pursues a course a little further to the south, crossing the hills to reach Princes Risborough on its recently extended service to Birmingham, with a little branch line from Princes Risborough which provides an alternative route to Aylesbury. Great Western Trains make a very brief visit to the very south of the county at Iver, and similarly the Virgin West Coast main line for just a mile or two south of Leighton Buzzard, beyond which Bucks is re-entered, passing through 'industrial' Bletchley, Milton Keynes and Wolverton (not recommended departure stations for country walks nowadays!). Sadly a veritable network of lines north of Aylesbury has disappeared, but rumours are rife that the link from Bletchley to Oxford may one day be revived. Thus the rural outpost of Verney Junction, once the northerly outpost of The Metropolitan Railway, might attain its day of resurrection.

The nine stations which the rambles within commence from and return to have been selected to show the diversity of scenery which Bucks offers. Whether you like the wooded grandeur of the Chilterns or the peace of the great vale, there is something to please. Buckinghamshire is truly an 'all the year round' county in which to ramble and the stations involved in this volume have a reasonable and daily rail service, a service which thanks to private enterprise has been much improved in the past couple of years.

PROLOGUE TO OXFORDSHIRE

Oxfordshire can be described as a 'buffer state' between the 'Home Counties' scenery of the Chiltern Hills and the distincly 'West Country' atmosphere of the Cotswolds. Between these lies a great basin, punctuated by hilly outcrops, the combination of which forms either the gathering ground or courses of the rivers that eventually precipitate into the mighty Thames. The highest point of the latter lies in the peaceful meadows just outside Oxfordshire's Dorchester where the River Thame joins the Isis. Hence the word Thames is formed.

In the great city of Oxford the Isis is fed by the waters of the Cherwell into which university students jump from the parapet of Magdalen Bridge in the early morning of May Day. North west of Oxford the River Evenlode emanates from Cotswold country as indeed does the Isis itself. The picturesquely named River Windrush has a similar derivation. A traveller coming from London to Oxfordshire via the M40 motorway will unobtrusively enter the country just before the great cutting that takes the highway down from the Chilterns to the vale in the neighbourhood of Lewknor village. Coming by rail, the county is entered when the line crosses a picturesque stretch of the Thames between Pangbourne and Goring.

What has hitherto been referred to as the plain is by no means flat, save for the peculiar tract of land known as Otmoor (visited in Walk Number 13). Even at the immediate east of Oxford city is a narrow and lofty ridge, the summit of which is known as Shotover Plain. The old village of Wheatley at the eastern end of the ridge displays a 'Cotswold' flavour. The county is bounded by Buckinghamshire, Northamptonshire, Cloucestershire, Warwickshire, Wiltshire and Berkshire. By way of comparitively recent boundary changes Oxfordshire 'poached' a corner of the great Vale of the White Horse, taking in such places as Didcot, Abingdon and Wallingford, etc.

Once the railway has crossed the Thames into the county, the main line to South Wales and the West Country pursues a course just below the Berkshire Downs until entering Wiltshire on its way to Swindon. The 'branch' at Didcot goes northward into Oxford where it 'trifurcates', the main artery going almost due north into Banbury *en route* for the Midlands. The right-hand branch just north of Oxford forms a shuttle service to Bicester, a recently resurrected passenger service which at present does not operate on Sundays. Plans are afoot to possibly upgrade this line to form part of a new high speed link between East Anglia and the south west. The left hand 'fork' on leaving Oxford forms what the railway company (Thames Trains) have dubbed The Cotswold Line. The eventual destination of this link is Hereford, passing Worcester and The Malverns on the way. It is interesting to note that Oxford is one of the halting points on Britain's longest journey without changing. Virgin Cross Country offer a daily service from Penzance to Dundee! Chiltern Railways from London (Marylebone) makes an incursion in and out of the county between Haddenham and Banbury.

Compiling a series of rambles suitable for a circular walk with a midway pub stop needs a measure of ingenuity. The five walks featured in this volume fulfil these qualifications. There are country stations between Didcot and Oxford (really rural places too) but due to the proximity of the river they do not lend themselves to anything resembling a circular walk. The Oxfordshire walks that have been selected depict a real diversity of the scenery that the county has to offer and one hopes that the reader will find them as enjoyable as the author and his wife did, when the material for the volume was being researched.

FOREWORD

Those who have seen the first volume of this series (dealing with Hertfordshire and Bedfordshire) will be aware of the concept of these rambles, i.e. that they are circular, starting and finishing at the same railway station with a 'pub stop' for refreshments at or about the half-way stage. In recent months there has been in the media and from government sources an entreaty to 'leave the car at home'. This is exactly what you can do if participating in these country walks, but of course you have the prerogative to use a car, preferably at week ends when station car parks are in the main almost empty.

Rambling became popular between the first and second world wars, when it was known as hiking, and has now become the most popular open air pastime. We are fortunate in this country to have a network of public footpaths (rights of way) making it possible to cover whole tracts of countryside without traversing public roads. In the early days of rambling the paths were often indistinct and, even with a good map, hard to follow, but nowadays the rights of way are signposted (and in some districts numbered) and at strategic points the route forward is indicated by waymarks often affixed to stiles and gates. Some schools of thought press for 'open access' to the countryside. Whilst respecting their right to hold these views, the author prefers the existing system. The rights of way are clearly indicated on Ordnance Survey 'Landranger' or 'Pathfinder' maps, and part of the enjoyment of country walking is to follow these as dilligently as possible, not knowing what will be around the next corner or over the next stile.

English country inns have undergone extensive changes within the last decade. Most of them offer 'bar snacks' or even full restaurant meals, generally at very reasonable prices. However this does not apply to all pubs . . . two really lovely country inns in this volume still serve only nuts and crisps, etc. Let this not deter the reader from visiting these hostelries . . . good ale with the aforementioned can still offer ample sustenance to enable the rambler to complete the return leg to the railway station.

Some pubs have rooms designated for the accommodation of children. Some do not, but if the weather is clement, there is always the alternative of the beer garden for the minors, and bear in mind that the inns that have catering facilities usually quote reduced prices on a special children's menu. For the non-drinker it is significant that apart from soft drinks, tea or coffee is nearly always available.

The walks in this volume vary in distance from 3½ to almost 8 miles. Care has been taken by the author to limit the traverse of public roads to the very minimum, and as far as possible to ensure that 'off road' sections follow designated rights of way. If by any chance you should accidentally stray from the prescribed route and are found on private land and confronted by the owner or his agent, humility should be the order of the day. The recommended approach is to explain that you have inadvertently strayed from the path and could you please be directed back to it.

On the subject of train fares, cheap day excursion tickets are currently available to all destinations in this book, provided that you are not starting out from a station which ss not a part of the 'Network South East' area (see datils on page 16). To reduce costs still further in the 'NSE' area you can purchase an annual 'Network Railcard' for the sum of £20. This will enable you to get a 35% discount off travel in the area at all times during Saturdays, Sundays, or Bank Holidays, or after 10am on weekdays. For 'cheap day' tickets without the Network Railcard, the weekday restriction is 9.30am. There is currently no restriction on the return journey times on weekdays but this situation might change at some time in the future . . . ask your local railway station for the latest information.

Rambling is an all the year round pastime. The frosts of winter can make the English countryside resemble Fairyland; in springtime the new foliage is a joy to behold; high summer proclaims its glory with an abundance of wild flowers; then we have the golden leaves of autumn. All seasons have their respective appeals. Remember too that except after long dry spells, you may encounter 'boggy' stretches, so therefore something in the way of protective footwear should be worn. The reader is also strongly recommended to buy the relevant maps (detailed in the 'factsheets'). If you are not skilled in map reading, you will soon acquire the art of 'translating' what you see on the map to the surrounding features. When you fully acquire the skill it opens up all sorts of possibilities for future excursions.

THE COUNTRY CODE

1. Avoid damage to fences, gates and walls. These are there for a purpose and to repair damage is often expensive.
2. Always close gates to prevent livestock escaping.
3. Keep to footpaths and other rights of way and avoid causing damage to crops.
4. Respect other people's property. Farm machinery is often left unattended close to where it is needed and should therefore be left untouched.
5. Keep dogs under control and if necessary keep them on a lead. If you cannot control your pet you should not take it out into the countryside. This applies not only where livestock is concerned but to many other areas. Rampaging dogs pose a serious threat to deer, especially when they have young, and desertion and even premature abortion sometimes result. Other wild mammals are disturbed as well as ground-nesting or ground-feeding birds.
6. Do not leave litter and especially do not discard lighted cigarettes, matches or anything else that could start a fire.
7. Drive slowly and safely in the country. Always assume that there might be a herd of cows or a stationary tractor round the next bend.
8. When walking on country roads always remember to keep to the right, in single file.

MUDDY FOOTWEAR

Publicans usually welcome ramblers. Accordingly it is right and proper that muddy shoes or boots should be removed before entry, therefore in the appropriate season it is wise to carry a pair of carpet slippers or plimsolls.

MAP SYMBOLS

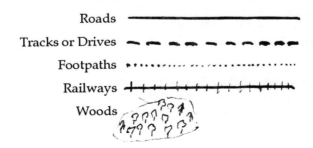

Roads

Tracks or Drives

Footpaths

Railways

Woods

WALKS SUMMARY

OXFORDSHIRE

ACCESS BY ROAD

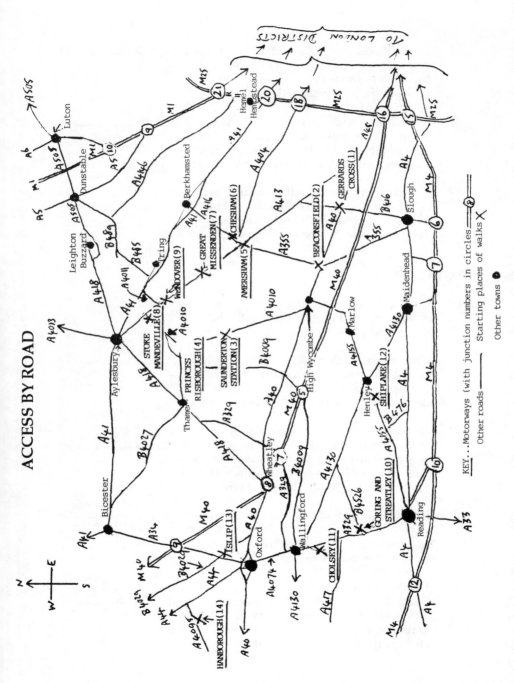

KEY...Motorways (with junction numbers in circles) ═══
Other roads ───
Starting places of walks ✕
Other towns ●

14

ACCESS BY RAIL

Walks commence at stations denoted by dark type, with the walk number in brackets following.

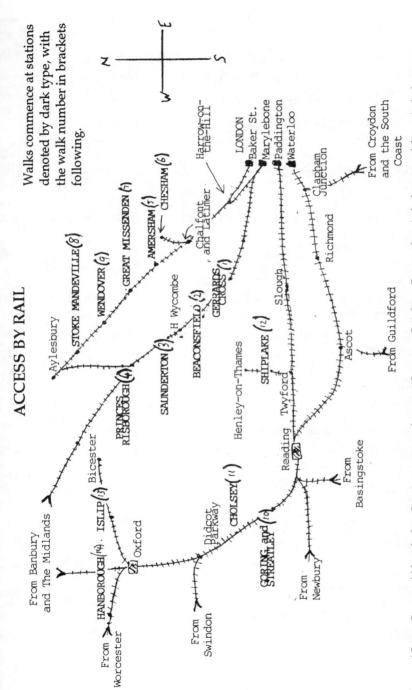

'Cross Country' bus links. Services operate between Luton or Leighton Buzzard to Aylesbury, and from Aylesbury on to Oxford. there is also a 'bus service operating from Berkhamsted to Chesham and Amersham. On Sundays the services may be very infrequent. Conversely a frequent service operates daily linking Harrow and Wealdstone station and Harrow-on-the-Hill. Otherwise from a northerly aspect it is more convenient to travel via London. Day return tickets usually include fares for an underground journey termini.

N.B. If using London Underground's Circle Line, Baker Street station is only a few minutes walk from Marylebone.

15

STATIONS TO AND FROM WHICH CHEAP DAY RETURN TICKETS AND 'NETWORK RAILCARDS' NORMALLY APPLY

ANY STATION in Kent, Sussex, Surrey Hampshire (including The Isle of Wight), Essex, Hertfordshire, Buckinghamshire, Oxfordshire, Doreset and Greater London.

CAMBRIDGESHIRE . . . all stations, *except* Peterborough, Whittlesey, March, Manea, Shippea Hill and Newmarket.

DEVON . . . stations between Axminster and Exeter St. Davids inclusive. Intermediate stations are Exeter Central, Pinhoe, Whimple, Feniton and Honiton.

GLOUCESTERSHIRE . . . Moreton-in-Marsh only.

HEREFORD AND WORCESTER . . . Honeybourne, Evesham, Pershore, Worcester (Shrub Hill) and Worcester (Foregate Street) only.

NORFOLK . . . Kings Lynn, Watlington and Downham Market only.

NORTHAMPTONSHIRE . . . Northampton and Long Buckby only.

SOMERSET . . . Templecombe, Yeovil Junction, Yeovil (Pen Mill) and Crewkerne only.

SUFFOLK . . . Bures and Sudbury only.

WILTSHIRE . . . Salisbury, Tisbury and Bedwyn only.

CHEAP DAY RETURN tickets are available at any time on Saturdays, Sunday, and public holidays. On other days the journey must commence after 9.30am, or 10.00am if a 'Network Railcard' is used.

N.B. The above facilities do not normally apply for 'internal' journeys from one London Underground station to another.

———————

SENIOR CITIZENS LIVING IN THE GREATER LONDON BOROUGHS . . . you currently have a travel permit giving free rail travel in the metropolitan boroughs. When travelling out of the area, there is no need to pay twice for the 'London' part of the journey. Ask for a day return ticket from Boundary Zone 6 to wherever you are travelling. Also note that the free rail concession applies outside the London area on the Chiltern or Metropolitan lines right out to Amersham or Chesham. If travelling beyond Amersham ask at any London Underground station or at Marylebone for an 'add on' ticket to Great Missenden, Wendover, Stoke Mandeville or Aylesbury . . . this will give the 'over 60s' a very cheap day out in the Chiltern Hills or Aylesbury Vale!

Walk 1

GERRARDS CROSS to 'the White Hart', THREE HOUSEHOLDS and back

<u>BY RAIL</u> . . . Gerrards Cross is on The Chiltern Line from London (Marylebone) to High Wycombe, Princes Risborough, (Aylesbury via a branch line), and Banbury, etc. Service up to 4 trains per hour, half hourly on Sundays.

<u>BY ROAD</u> . . . From London area, A40 to Gerrards Cross Common. Turn right on common. Station and car park are on the left after passing over railway bridge. From a northerly direction, leave M1 at junction 8, thence through Hemel Hempstead town to Boxmoor (on A4251). After passing under bridges go left via B4505 to Chesham and on to Amersham, A355 to Beaconsfield. Turn left at Beaconsfield town centre and follow A40 for 3½ miles to Gerrards Cross Common, where turn left for station and car park.

<u>MAP</u> . . . Ordnance Survey Landranger Sheet 176.

<u>DISTANCE OF WALK</u> . . . Approximately 6½ miles.

<u>TOPOGRAPHY</u> . . . When the River Colne is crossed approaching Denham, one is in Buckinghamshire and the subsequent rising ground marks the very beginning of the 'Chiltern' ridges. Indeed a suburban street and pub in Uxbridge town are somewhat optimistically named 'Chiltern View'. The slightly higher ground around Gerrards Cross forms a sort of 'table land', a buffer state between the mainly flat landscape of Middlesex and the Chiltern uplands to the west. Nothing daunting in the way of hill climbs is encountered on this walk. An interesing feature of this locality is the number of 'enclosed' footpaths, threading their way through the countryside between hedges and fences and in some cases walls.

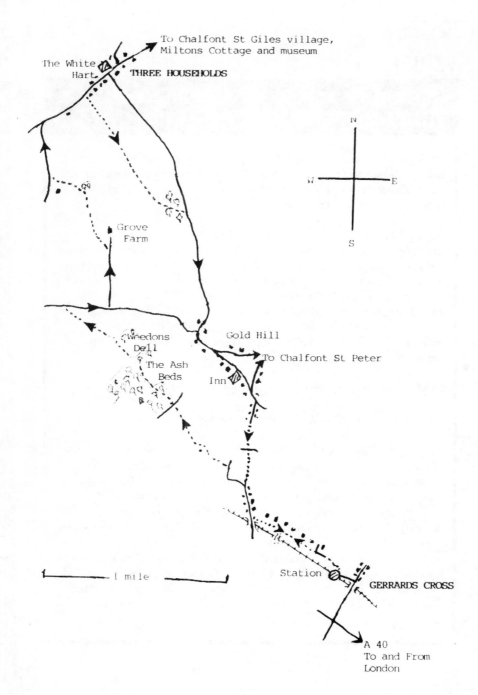

To Chalfont St Giles village,
Miltons Cottage and museum

The White
Hart

THREE HOUSEHOLDS

N

W —— E

S

Grove
Farm

Weedons
Dell

Gold Hill

To Chalfont St Peter

The Ash
Beds

Inn

1 mile

Station

GERRARDS CROSS

A 40
To and From
London

18

GERRARDS CROSS was originally the name of the cross roads on the A40 road in the middle of the common. Around are some comparatively old dwellings and a fine inn, the Pack Horse. At the turn of the century, the country's newest main line railway, the Great Central, was built through Gerrard's Cross on its route from Northern England to London's new terminal, Marylebone. The line ran north of the common land, beyond which was well wooded ground with little habitation. With the advent of the railway things changed rapidly. With a shopping street as a nucleus, a high class commuter belt developed. Today these tree-lined roads largely consisting of detached properties, contain amongst their denizens a good proportion of medical consultants, stockbrokers, and those whose faces are familiar in or on the popular media.

On leaving the station go across the yard and left uphill along a tarred path which soon joins a small road. Ahead where the road goes to the right keep ahead along another tarred passageway ignoring left and right turnings, emerging in some half mile into a by-road. Here turn to the right, passing Gayhurst School on the left, then going left at a road junction into Maltmans Lane. After the lane bears round to the right and opposite a house named Oak Manor, turn left at a footpath sign along an enclosed path that soon leads out into a tarred farm drive. Go forward along the drive. In about 300 yards at a dip keep right along an enclosed path with farm buildings on the left, beyond which the path returns to the tarred drive. Where the drive goes off to the right, keep forward along a delightful little enclosed path, which after crossing another path at right angles leads out into a minor road.

Cross this road and a few paces to the left turn right along a track through wooded ground. After some 200 yards go through a wooden swing gate. The path runs ahead in the same forward direction firstly on the right hand side of woods and then entering woodland known as The Ash Beds. The path takes a slight turn of direction to the left and on a downward gradient. Where you see the end of the wood ahead aim for a gap into a meadow, where follow the direction of electricity poles. After soon 100 yards on your right is . . .

WEEDONS DELL, a deep hollow in a belt of woodland. The origin of these hollows, which abound in this and neighbouring areas is lost in the midst of antiquity. They are most probably the remains of ancient quarries.

Having passed the dell on your right aim leftwards for about 40 yards and observe the remains of an old stile and gate. Proceed ahead, firstly with trees on the left and open ground on the right. Cross a stile and keep in roughly the same direction through what appears to be the remains of an iron gate. The path now becomes enclosed and goes through a dip emerging into . . .

WELDERS LANE, a narrow country lane with passing places for traffic. The lane is used often as a short cut, so proceed carefully as motor traffic jostles for position at the passing bays. Generally it is safer to walk on the right in these circumstances.

Turn right into the lane and after about a third of a mile, turn left along a private drive to Grove Farm. About 150 yards before reaching the farmhouse go left over a substantial stile and proceed diagonally to the corner of the field with outbuildings to your right and along the left hand side of a field to a crossroads of paths. Go forward here over rough pasture to a clear stile ahead, leading into a thicket of bushes. The path winds clearly through the dense vegetation, the only hazard being the rabbit burrows which intrude, for this is a place with a large rabbit population, as you might have guessed before entering the thicket. You emerge into a made up farm drive which follow out into a secondary road where turn right. Follow this road for some three-quarters of a mile to the hamlet of . . .

THREE HOUSEHOLDS (which is also the name of the road), a settlement of mainly modern dwellings on the perimeter of Chalfont St. Giles. The origin of the name is obvious but there has been much multiplication this century! On your left is . . .

THE WHITE HART, a modernish sort of inn from its outside appearance but very cosy and friendly inside. Morlands of Abingdon provide the ales (augmented by a guest beer). A wide variety of bar meals and snacks are available. From literature on the notice boards, etc. one can assume that the pub has a close association with the nearby village cricket ground.

(To visit Milton's Cottage and museum continue past The White Hart for about half a mile, beyond which is the centre of Chalfont St. Giles village.)

Leaving the inn, retrace your incoming route for a short quarter mile. After passing (on the left) a house called The Beams, turn left along a clear and enclosed path between the ground now occupied by Chalfont Park Golf Course. After about a mile the path emerges at a clearing with a wooden fence on your right. Proceed forward to join another path which runs just inside some wooded ground where bear left, soon emerging into a road.

This is Narcot Lane, which follow straight on. At a sharpish left hand bend, the road becomes known as Grove Lane. Ahead you soon reach the western fringe of . . .

GOLD HILL COMMON, an undulating stretch of grass, gorse and woodland set between a triangle of three minor roads. At the lower apex of the common land is the village of Chalfont St. Peter in the Misbourne Valley. Facing the common and on your right is a commodious pub, the not too distantly rebuilt 'Jolly Farmers'.

Having passed by the aforementioned, take the second turning on the right, Austinwood Close. Where the road ends go forwards along a tarred passageway with a Roman Catholic school on the right. Crossing a local road the path continues on (with Gerrards Cross Bowling Club on the left). You emerge at the corner of Maltmans Lane, from where you retrace the outward route along Bulls Lane, turning left before the railway bridge and so back to Gerrards Cross Station.

Walk 2

BEACONSFIELD Station to The Red Lion, PENN and back

<u>BY RAIL</u> . . . Beaconsfield is served by The Chiltern Line from Marylebone Station in London. Frequent service on weekdays and Saturdays. Half-hourly on Sundays. From the opposite direction the service runs from Birmingham, Banbury, High Wycombe and Aylesbury, etc.

<u>BY ROAD</u> . . . From London area, A40, then M40 to junction 2, where turn off for Beaconsfield town centre. near far end of High Street, turn right. Railway station is some three-quarters ahead on your right. From a northerly aspect, leave M1 at junction 8 thence through Hemel Hempstead town centre to join A4251. Passing under arches at Boxmoor, take B4505 to Chesham then on to Amersham, where follow A355. One mile short of Beaconsfield turn right along unclassified road. On reaching B474 turn left. Station is ¼ mile on on your left.

<u>MAP</u> . . . Ordnance Survey Pathfinder Sheet 175 or Explorer Sheet 3.

<u>DISTANCE OF WALK</u>. . . Approximately 6 miles.

<u>TOPOGRAPHY</u> . . . The region visited in this walk can be described as 'Traditional Chiltern Country'. There is a succession of rolling hills, beech woods and dry valleys. Little wonder that the region has been designated an 'Area of Outstanding Beauty'. From the beginning of the walk you are gently rising to the ridge on which the village of Penn stands. Glorious views abound hereabouts, perhaps seen at their best when the autumn is turning the leaves to gold. You will hardly notice the gradual ascent and indeed the only gradient of note is near the end of the walk, a dip after leaving the hamlet of Forty Green, a sharp rise of some 75 feet. The paths hereabouts are well used and are in reasonably good condition at all times of the year.

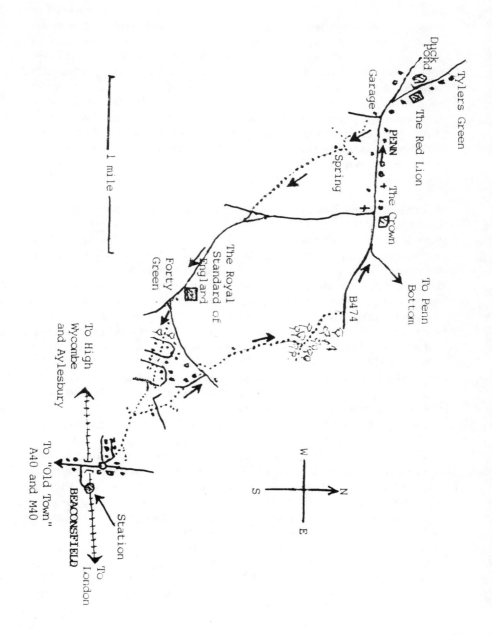

23

BEACONSFIELD, like Amersham, a few miles to the north, has become almost two separate towns. Around the railway station is the 'new town' which grew up as a commuter centre. It contains a shopping street dating back to the thirties, a supermarket, and quiet residential roads which radiate in all directions. Some quarter of a mile from the station in an extensive house garden is the renowned model railway complete with village known as Bekonscot. To visit this leave the station on the north side and follow signposts. Some three-quarters of a mile to the south is the old town with picturesque buildings straddling the main A40 road. Happily to say the old town centre is much quieter than it used to be following the construction of the M40 motorway a little further to the south.

Leave the station by the ramp road and on reaching the main street turn right. After a few yards you come to a roundabout. Here fork to your left along Reynolds Road keeping to the right hand pavement. The road soon bends to the left. Here continue straight on along a little enclosed alley which after some 30 yards leads into a 'green way' which is fenced and runs behind back gardens. After some 400 yards you come to a junction of ways. Here turn sharp right and having done so rightwards again, ignoring the path which veers off to the left. This enclosed way (which continues to run between the back gardens of opulent properties) eventually crosses a road. A little further on the path forks. Here take the left hand path which runs ahead with some wooded ground on your right and out into a quiet residential road. Follow this road for some 200 yards out into an older road, where turn left.

After just a short way turn right on to a footpath which runs by a hedge, with allotments on your right. The path soon takes a leftwards direction and for a few yards becomes enclosed, soon opening out to a point with a stile ahead. Cross this stile and go half right to another stile about 20 yards ahead continuing slightly uphill along a long narrow field. Passing over the next stile the path follows the right hand side of the next field with something resembling a derelict pavilion on your left. The next stile leads into some bushy ground and the clear path soon descends into a dip in which the route continues forward and rightwards into some woods, very soon coming to a T-junction of fenced paths where turn left. On emerging from the woods the path keeps ahead for a little way and then veers to the right with the hedge on your right. At the corner of the field the path becomes enclosed and leads ahead, emerging in some 100 yards into a 'secondary' road, the B474. Here turn to your left. This road can be quite busy and it is recommended that you cross to the right hand side where for much of the way there is an ample grass verge to take refuge. The road bends and rises. To the left opens out a vista in the direction of the Thames Valley. It is said that Windsor Castle can be seen on a clear day. To your right the backdrop is delightful . . . you look across Penn Bottom to the vast woodland beyond. You are entering the village of

PENN set high upon a Chiltern ridge. On your left is the parish church. William Penn, the founder of far away Pennsylvania lived nearby and four of his grandchildren are buried in the churchyard. On your right you pass (or visit?) a fine old inn, The Crown.

The road beyond the inn has a pavement and following this for a good half mile (passing *en route* the Free Methodist Church). Just after passing a garage on the left the 'B' road veers off to the left. Here keep straight on along a lesser road. In a few moments you reach on your right . . .

THE RED LION. PENN.

25

THE RED LION, an exceptionally friendly old pub with ample selections of fine food and a choice of no less than 7 cask beers. It is worthwhile strolling a few yards beyond The Red Lion as hereabouts is an exceptionally large duck pond, well populated with ducks!

Leaving The Red Lion, retrace your steps to the 'B' road and at the garage now on your right turn right down a narrowish lane. After some 200 yards turn left along a drive signposted to a house named Thatchers Field. You soon reach a point where the way ahead is barred. At this point you emerge into a bridleway where turn right descending to a dip. Ignore a stile on your right but a few yards on at the junction of bridlepaths go right (still descending) and having passed some wet ground around a spring the way continues clearly between hedges for three-quarters of a mile to emerge eventually at a junction of tiny roads. Cross to the far road and follow this, descending into a valley to join another metalled but narrow lane. Follow this through the valley eventually rising to the hamlet of ...

FORTY GREEN, a tiny outpost of Beaconsfield best known for its capacious inn, the renowned Royal Standard of England. It is reputed that Marstons Brewery produced their strong tipple, Owd Roger, specially for this inn, although nowadays this delectable brew is available in various other selected outlets.

As you pass the entrance to the pub on your left take the right hand fork of the two roads and descend for a couple of hundred yards to a further meeting of minor roads. Here take the left hand option, ascending quite steeply. After some 50 yards go to the right along a footpath which slants across open ground and through a dip and up into a belt of trees. Ignore a crossing path and continue by the enclosed way which crosses three quiet residential roads. On reaching the fourth road, go right for a few yards and then left into a side road, Malkin Drive. Where this short road ends go to the right and follow the line of another enclosed alley which soon leads out into a junction of similar paths. Here go right and the immediately left. You have, as you may recognise, rejoined your outward route, so take the first path on your right and out into the roundabout by Beaconsfield station.

Walk 3

SAUNDERTON STATION to The Pink and Lily, PARSLOWS HILLOCK, and back

BY RAIL . . . Chiltern Railways from London Marylebone, via Wembley (Stadium), West Ruislip, and High Wycombe, etc. Hourly service. In other directions trains calling at Saunderton originate at Aylesbury.

BY ROAD . . . From London area, A40, then M40 to junction 4, where follow A4010 to Saunderton station, entrance to which is immediately on left after passing Golden Cross pub. From northerly aspect, see walk number 8, and having passed Stoke Mandeville station carry on upon A4010 through Princes Risborough, three miles beyond which is turning to Saunderton station on right.

MAP . . . Ordnance Survey Landranger sheet number 165 or Explorer sheets 2 and 3.

DISTANCE . . . Approximately 6¼ miles.

TOPOGRAPHY . . . This is by way of altitude the highest walk in the volume. The outgoing route is nearly all on an uphill gradient, and after the pub stop it is nearly all down. The spur of the Chiltern Hills that towers above Princes Risborough is amongst the classic scenic routes of South-East England. There are places with higher altitudes in Surrey and Berkshire, but the vista from the neighbourhood of Parslows Hillock is more extensive. It may be an apocryphal story that parts of Wales can be seen, but certainly when the outlook is clear, the Malvern Hills on the borders of Herefordshire and Worcestershire are visible. On the whole the underfoot conditions are good, but be prepared – the bridleway from Kiln Lane, Lacey Green to Lily Bottom Lane soon becomes extremely soft after rainfall.

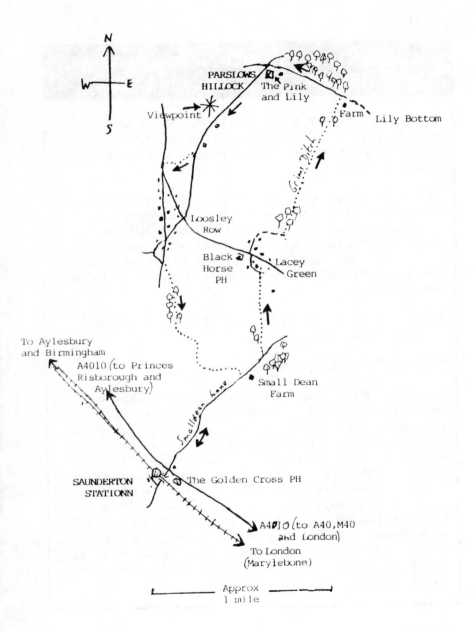

SAUNDERTON STATION, let it be stressed is not in Saunderton! It is a good 3 miles from Saunderton village, which in turn is only some half mile from Princes Risborough station. A theory relating to the apparent anomoly is that the site of Saunderton station is at a locality known as Slough. Presumably the railway company did not wish intending passengers to confuse it with 'big' Slough which also used to be in Buckinghamshire until it was, some years ago, moved overnight into the bounds of neighbouring Berkshire. That still does not explain why Saunderton was chosen as the (misleading) name. Perhaps Smalldean or Slough Bottom Lane would have been more appropriate.

Leave Saunderton station via the descending drive at the end of which turn left under the railway bridge. At the crossroads ahead (The Golden Cross pub is on your immediate right) go forward into Smalldean Lane, a byway which soon becomes both narrow and twisting. Ignoring two footpaths on your left, you ascend gradually and then after a brief descent pass picturesque Small Dean Farm on your right, and a little further on a small car park and picnic area on the verge of the National Trust land around the nearby village of Bradenham. Shortly after this and as the lane begins to ascend seriously, take a left hand turn, through a swing gate along a path which ascends along the right hand side of a field.

At the corner of the field the path goes through another swing gate and becomes a green way with a little wood on your left, after which it becomes enclosed with a hedgerow on one side and a wire fence on the other. Breasting the top of the prolonged rising ground, you cross a farm track after which the path soon ends upon joining a quiet road, where turn to your left. The road bends round rightwards and enters a secondary road. The scattered village which you are traversing is . . .

LACEY GREEN . . perched high upon a spur of The Chilterns, this community loftily looks down on neighbouring countryside. The author recalls in years following World War 2, that a 'private' omnibus service operated hereby on a somewhat circumlocutory route from Princes Risborough to High Wycombe. The single decker 'bus was well (and sometimes) overpatronised. The local people referred to it as 'The Farmers' Jam Service'!

On entering the secondary road, turn left for a few yards and then turn right along Kiln Lane. (A few yards beyond the turning into Kiln Lane and on the left is The Black Horse pub.) Kiln Lane is designated as a 'no through road' and soon the tarred surface gives way to an 'unmetalled' state. After the lane steeply descends and takes a sharpish turn to the right, you come to a crossing of rights of way. Turn left here on to a bridle path that steeply climbs through a belt of trees. This is the site of . . .

GRIMS DITCH . . . an earthwork that wends its way across Chiltern country. Its origin is unknown. It is certainly prehistoric, and some theories proclaim that it was a tribal boundary, others subscribe to the view that it was built to keep out unwanted animals.

The bridle path continues forward for a full mile, at the end of which it descends abruptly into Lily Bottom, with farm buildings on your right. Turn left here along the tarred Lily Bottom Lane. In a short half mile you come to a junction of roads at . . .

PARSLOWS HILLOCK . . . an isolated high-up meeting place of roads at the very edge of The Chiltern Escarpment.

At the junction of roads, turn left into Pink Road. Immediately to your left is . . .

THE PINK AND LILY pub, much extended these days with dining areas and alcoves augmented by a large beer garden. A variety of good cask ales are available, including refreshing (low gravity) ales from Flowers or Brakspears breweries. A guest ale, usually of higher strength, is normally available. The choice of food is abundant, ranging from a snack from the starter menu to a full restaurant meal. A nice feature herein is that when food is ordered you are not given a numbered ticket. The bar staff ask for your forename which is called out when your order is ready. When the author visited the Pink and Lily on a busy sunny Sunday, the food was produced with commendable alacrity. A tiny bar in the old part of the pub is named The Brooke Bar. The Pub was a favourite venue of the early 20th century poet, Rupert Brooke, who died so tragically when serving his country in World War 1. His picture adorns the inn signs.

Inn sign depicting Rupert-Brooke.

Leaving the pub continue along Pink Road. After some 300 yards a spectacular view on your right becomes apparent. This surely is the place where Rupert Brooke in his poem, The Chilterns, related to:

> White mists about the black hedgerows
> The slumbering Midland plain.

Having passed an equestrian centre and a farm entrance on your left look out for a footpath sign on your right. The path goes diagonally across a field and then having crossed two stiles (close together) goes downhill along the left hand edge of the next field, over two more adjacent stiles and rightwards through a bank of trees and steeply down to a few steps which lead into a road. Here turn to your left. In a fork of the road right ahead, take the right hand option, Lower Road. With more views across the low ground on your right you pass through the straggling village of . . .

LOOSLEY ROW, a place set upon the hillside, a sort of 'buffer state' twixt The Chilterns and The Great Vale. The long obsolete 'bus

31

service, referred to in the notes about Lacey Green, also served this village.

Continuing along Lower Road you come to a crossroads where go straight on, ignoring a footpath sign indicating a path on your left. Soon another small road emerges from your right. Opposite this road junction is another footpath sign. Take this path which rises gently along the left hand side of a field, at the end of which cross a stile and keeping in the same direction follow the way through a belt of woodland. Where the path emerges from the trees, there is another stile which appears presently to be superfluous, as currently there is a large 'gap' to go through. The path goes ahead across a field with the hedge on your left, and over another stile into a very large field. Just follow the left hand margin of this which, after bending to the right and then to the left, brings you back to Smalldean Lane (featured on the outward journey). Turn right here and retrace your steps for some three-quarters of a mile to the cross roads and under bridge to Saunderton station.

'The slumbering Midland Plain'.

Walk 4

PRINCES RISBOROUGH to 'the Lions of Bledlow', BLEDLOW, and back

BY RAIL . . . Princes Risborough is on the main Chiltern line service from London (Marylebone) to Banbury and Birmingham. Semi-fast trains operate ½ hourly on weekdays and Saturdays. Slower trains on hourly basis on Sundays.

BY ROAD . . . From London Area – M40 to junction 4, thence on to A4010 to a point about 1 mile short of Princes Risborough where bear left on to B4441. Princes Risborough station is three-quarters of a mile further on. From a northerly aspect, leave junction 11 of M1 (between Luton and Dunstable). Passing through Dunstable follow B489 to Ivinghoe thence B485 to join A41 where turn right towards Aylesbury. In just over 1 mile left on to B4544 and A4010 to Princes Risborough. Alternatively leave M25 at junction 18, then A404 through Amersham to High Wycombe, then westwards on A40 and A4010 to point just outside Princes Risborough where follow B4441 to station.

MAP . . . Ordnance Survey Pathfinder Sheet 165 or Explorer Sheet 2.

DISTANCE OF WALK . . . Approximately 5½ miles.

TOPOGRAPHY . . . This ramble is typical Buckinghamshire territory – just within the pastures of The Aylesbury Vale, with the heights of The Chilterns to the south. Being not very far from the boundary with Oxfordshire, you are close to the watershed where some streams meander south-westwards to eventually join the Thames and some north-easterly to the region of the Cambridgeshire Ouse. The paths are well used and are in reasonably good condition all the year round. The Lyde at Bledlow is a unique geographical feature (see text of ramble) and a short diversion into its depths is, if one may say so, obligatory. As for gradients, they are negligable. Although the surrounding country is by no means flat, the highest point of the walk at Bledlow village is no more than 100 feet above the start.

33

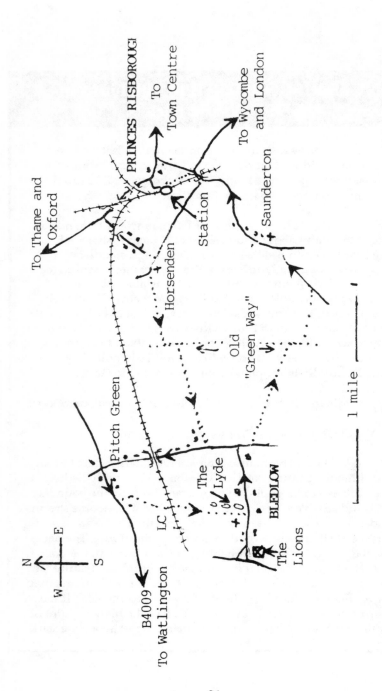

PRINCES RISBOROUGH is at the foot of the Chiltern Escarpment at a point where the main road from High Wycombe to Aylesbury crossed the ancient Icknield Way. The town centre is to an extent unspoiled, but like all towns within commuting distance of London it is encircled with a 'rash' of modern development. The railway station and its adjacent car park are some three-quarters of a mile from the main shopping streets. The town is a gateway to the great Vale of Aylesbury with associated extensive pastures and in most instances duck ponds adjoining the farmhouses. Like most places on the outer periphery of the London area, it is indeed a quiet haven for those who have spent the day amid the maelstrom of The City. At one time Princes Risborough was a major railway junction, with branches from the main line (to Birmingham, Birkenhead, etc.) leading off to Oxford (via Thame), to Watlington and to Aylesbury. Only the latter now remains, although part of the Watlington line has been resurrected by steam and/or vintage enthusiasts.*

Leaving Princes Risborough station by the main exit, turn left in the yard and then right to join the main road, (to visit the town centre turn right here). For the ramble turn left. Across the road are a few shops, once of which sells models . . . a glance at their shop window will reveal some nostalgic railway scenes, etc. Forward, you soon pass under two railway bridges. Then in some 50 yards, go to your left as signposted to Princes Industrial Estate. After passing the light industrial buildings keep ahead over three stiles in fairly quick succession, emerging into a tiny road at . . .

HORSENDEN, a really remote hamlet consisting of a farm, a manor house, and the delightfully situated church. There is no way out for vehicular traffic from Horsenden, for the one road is a dead end. Different it was in the past, for at one time long years ago the lane constituted part of one of the main routes from London to Oxford.

Turn right on entering the lane and pass the church on your left. Where the dead end lane goes sharply away to the right (note the warning sign that there is not even a turning place at its end,) go ahead over a stile and shortly another and keep in a forward course

---

* Since going to press, plans are mooted for a revival of regular trains to serve a 'parkway' at Aston Rowant close to the M40 direct to London (Marylebone).

along the clear path which soon emerges into the remains of an old green lane. Turn left in the lane for some 30 yards and then emerge rightwards on to a path with the hedge on your left. In some half mile you pass farm buildings on your right and emerge into a road. Turn right here and descend, soon passing under a railway arch. Nearby was the site of . . .

BLEDLOW BRIDGE HALT, a tiny wayside station without raised platforms and just long enough to accommodate one carriage. The author recalls a day in the late forties when an eight-coach 'Ramblers Special' train from Paddington called here. The guard was diligent in seeing that all patrons for this halt where shepherded into the front carriage for descent, which was made possible by a short step ladder kept within the train. The days of 'Ramblers Specials' are long gone but in the author's memory they remain. Will they ever return? On the credit side this stretch of the line has been kept open by enthusiasts, and you might if your are fortunate to witness the rumble of a steam train.

Having passed the bridge you come in a short while to a crossroads at . . .

PITCH GREEN, one of the 'outposts' of Bledlow, of which there are also nearby the picturesquely named Holly Green, Forty Green and Skittle Green. There used to be a pub at Pitch Green, but it is no more.

Turn left at the cross roads and follow the B4009 road for a short quarter of a mile to a point on your left where there is a double footpath sign. Take the path that follows the hedge on your immediate right. After some 75 yards go right though a kissing gate, then leftwards with trees and the hedge now on your left. The clear path goes ahead and crosses the resurrected railway by means of a 'stop, look and listen' crossing. Having passed a house on your left the path becomes enclosed and ascends with a valley on your left. This valley is known as . . .

THE LYDE, a deep and steep cleft in the hillside where cool clear water gushes out of springs. The area is quite unique, and in recent years has been 'landscaped', with paths winding hither and thither, and seats to rest on. In high summer, the atmosphere is that of a tropical garden.

The footpath emerges into the churchyard and so into a road, where turn right. You are now in the centre of ...

BLEDLOW, a spread-out parish with 'satellite' hamlets within its perimeter. The church is impressive, and seems to be large enough to suit a small town rather than a village. Ahead you will see rising hills, in the slopes of which is carved in the chalk a huge cross, which only becomes visible from a point further along.

In a few yards you emerge on the village green. On your right is ...

THE LIONS OF BLEDLOW, a pub with ample room within and plenty of cosy 'alcoves' to enjoy your fare. Good ales are food are available and in the right climatic conditions beer tables are delightfully positioned on the green itself, as is the inn sign. No main route passes the site of 'The Lions' – it is a meeting place of unclassified lanes, bridleways, and footpaths.

The Lions of Bledlow

Retrace your steps after leaving the pub and follow the road with the church and the gate into The Lyde on your left. In a quarter mile you come to a T-junction, where turn right. After passing a few houses on your left, take a left hand turning into a path that runs rightwards and diagonally across a sizeable field. Arriving at the hedge you re-enter the old green lane that was encountered on the outward journey. Turn right in the green lane and after a matter of some 25 yards emerge on your left to a clear path that soon picks up the line of some farm buildings and becomes tarred. On joining a minor road, keep forward and on reaching a junction, go left. The church and buildings (some old and some new) constitute the village of ...

SAUNDERTON. As you enter the locality you may well hear the rushing of water in ditches, for this is a gathering ground for streams that emerge into the clay of the vale from their underground channels in the chalk hills. A peculiar thing about Saunderton is that it is nearly three miles from the railway station of the same name. Conversely if you want to go to Saunderton by train, alight at Princes Risborough ... only half a mile away! The possible explanation is that Saunderton Station is at a hamlet called Slough ... the railway companies obviously did not desire any confusion with *the* Slough, some fifteen miles to the south-east!

Inn sign and tables on the green.

To complete the walk continue along the road until you come to a junction of ways by a railway bridge. Go to the right across the bridge and, having done so, immediately turn left down a few steps and follow the ensuing enclosed alleyway into Princes Risborough station yard.

Walk 5

AMERSHAM to 'the Red Lion', LITTLE MISSENDEN, and back

BY RAIL . . . Chiltern trains from London (Marylebone) station via Harrow on the Hill and Rickmansworth to Amersham. Thereafter through Wendover to Aylesbury. At least 2 trains per hour. *IMPORTANT NOTE* – On Sundays the Chiltern Trains only rarely run between London and Amersham*. The alternative service is by London Underground from Baker Street. On Sundays a shuttle service at hourly intervals operates between Amersham and Aylesbury.

BY ROAD . . . From London and the south, A40 to Denham roundabout, thence via A416 to Amersham Old Town, where turn right on A416 to Amersham station. The northerly approach is via A41 turning off south of Berkhamsted on to A416 through Chesham.

MAPS . . . Ordnance Survey Landranger Sheet 165 or Ordnance Survey Explorer Sheet 3.

DISTANCE OF WALK . . . Approximately 5½ miles.

TOPOGRAPHY . . . Starting on a ridge above the valley of the little Misbourne River, the route goes in and out of wooded ground, descending sharply approaching Little Missenden village. Returning amidst parkland adjoining the river to the lovely old High Street of Amersham (Old Town), the route concludes with a formidable rise to rejoin the ridge at Amersham Station. Being in the heart of the Chiltern Hills, this is popular rambling country and the paths are clear and simple to follow.

* *Improvements promised from 1998.*

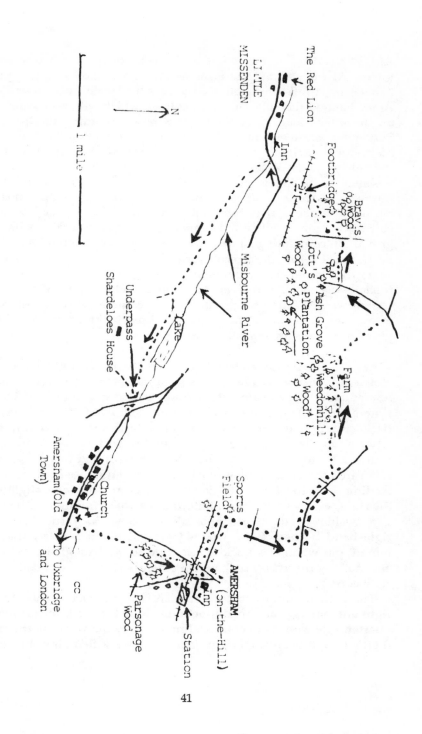

AMERSHAM has in the course of this century become two separate towns. At the station, one is in what is now known as just plain Amersham. Until comparatively recently the locality was designated Amersham-on-the-Hill. The original town which will be encountered on the return journey of the walk is now, according to Ordnance Survey maps, Amersham Old Town. The reason for all this is that the Metropolitan Railway from London had to cross a high ridge between the valleys of the River Colne and the Misbourne River. It was not possible for the line to descend quick enough to serve the old town centre, a distance of almost a mile away and with a difference of altitude of some two hundred feet. The station was therefore constructed on a hill amidst open country. Inevitably, with the growth of 'commuting', a new town sprung up in the purlieus of the railway. The result, the typical 'thirties' suburb that we have today. Its somewhat mundane shopping streets are surrounded by quiet side roads with mainly opulent properties. Until World War 2, the commuter who found success in The City could if he so wished travel to work each day in a Pullman Car for the price of a first class ticket, plus a nominal supplement.

Leaving the station go left down the station yard, right at the Iron Horse pub, then after a few yards left into Rectory Lane, and almost immediately right again into a quiet cul-de-sac, Longfield Drive. Where the road ends, turn right along a path which skirts a playing field, crosses two roads and leads into a third road where turn left. After about half a mile and immediatley past house number 51, follow a narrow path on the left through trees and bushes. After a few yards the path becomes enclosed between house gardens, soon leading out into a field. At this point the clear path veers slightly to the right, with woods ahead. Entering the wood through a stile (or a gap beside it) the path runs ahead some 30 yards from the right-hand border of the wooded ground. Soon a forest track is joined, but when this track bends right to go through a gate, keep ahead along the grassy path which emerges from the wood at its far right corner.

The path continues across a largish field veering slightly to the right and emerges at a road junction, where turn left. In just over a quarter mile woods are entered. Immediately the wood on the right (Lott's Wood) begins, go right on a rough track that almost follows the right of the wood. The path leads on with a hedge on the left, soon emerging at a tiny road. Cross this road to a drive opposite, signposted to Keepers Cottage. A short way ahead the drive bends to the left towards the cottage. Here proceed ahead along a clear path which descends steeply through the trees. On leaving the wood bear left to cross a lattice footbridge over the railway, after which the enclosed path descends by the railway, turns sharp left and leads into the main road. Cross this main road with due care and follow a 'lesser' road which passes The Crown Pub and shortly to the centre of ...

LITTLE MISSENDEN, still living up to its name. Little it was and little it is, probably on account of the fact that although The Metropolitan Railway built the line only quarter of a mile to the north, no station was ever planned. The village, happily to say, is 'by-passed' and is not disturbed by through traffic. It is verily one of the gems of The Chilterns, a peaceful meeting place of minor roads, a fine old church, pretty cottages, and a couple of real country pubs.

THE RED LION is at the village centre, backed by the waters of The Misbourne River, which at this point has been 'canalised' into a rustic duck pond. A variety of good food is served at the bar on every day of

the year except Christmas Day. Cask ales include Benskins or Hook Norton Bitters and Morlands' (of Abingdon) 'Old Speckled Hen'.

Leaving the pub retrace your steps past The Crown. Shortly the road bears to the left. At this point go to the right over a stile by a gate and follow a drive. The main drive turns left in about half a mile. At this point the way lies ahead with a hedge on your right. Cross an old hedged lane and quarter of a mile further on where the track veers right up to some woods, go slightly left along a grassy path which soon skirts an artificial lake. This is ...

SHARDELOES PARK and the mansion will be seen on the hill on your right. The house was built in the latter part of the eighteenth century for the then local member of Parliament.

The path continues through a gate and out on to a cricket field, which cross to lodge gates on the far side. Leaving the gates go ahead on a small metalled path, which accompanied by the Misbourne, goes under the by-pass road. The path runs along the left side of the road for a few yards and then winds to the left to join the 'old' road which soon becomes the High Street of ...

Little Missenden village street.

AMERSHAM (Old Town), unspoiled even today, with its cafes, restaurants, little pubs and larger coaching inns. It has a fine old parish church, adjoining a peaceful memorial garden, and, close to the old market hall, an arcade of little shops. No modern shopping mall intrudes and even a well-known supermarket lies unobtrusively at the far easterly end of the High Street. Whether you need a coffee, a beer or a meal it is a place to linger in, surely one of the most unspoiled town centres with a 25 mile radius of Central London.

Continue into the High Street, and having passed the church, turn left into the memorial garden. On emerging from the garden bear left and then right and follow a clear metalled path which ascends quite steeply to enter Parsonage Wood, where follow the main path ahead which eventually veers to the left into Rectory Lane, which follow under a railway bridge to join the outgoing route at the junction with Longfield Drive. Turn right, then left by The Iron Horse pub to the station yard.

Walk 6

CHESHAM to 'the Five Bells', near BOTLEY, and back

BY RAIL . . . London Underground (Metropolitan Line) from Baker Street. Most services originate at Aldgate passing Liverpool Street, Kings Cross and Euston Square, etc. Change at Chalfont and Latimer for shuttle service to Chesham. From a north-west direction Chiltern Line trains start from Aylesbury to Chalfont and Latimer. Services at least ½ hourly everyday, except Aylesbury line which is hourly on Sundays, upon which day you will also be obliged to change at Amersham.

BY ROAD . . . From London area A41 (reached by junction 20 from M25), thence via A416 into Chesham. From north leave M1 at junction 8, and follow A414 to A41 and thereafter A416. Alternatively through Dunstable, then B489. Leave B489 after some 3 miles annd follow B4506 to Berkhamsted. Turn right along A4251 to town ventre, thence A416 into Chesham.

MAP . . . Ordnance Survey Pathfinder Sheet 165 or Explorer Sheet 2.

DISTANCE OF WALK . . . Approximately 4 miles.

TOPOGRAPHY . . . Up into the hills from the Chess Valley and close to the Hertfordshire border. Such a delightful tract of country on the lower reaches of the Chilterns. Yes, there is a very steep climb some few minutes after starting the walk, but thereafter the undulations are anything but steep, save for the 'plunge' back to the valley right at the end. This, the shortest walk in the series so far, is even suitable for a summer evening, particularly with City workers, for the train service is frequent until quite late, (there are even a couple of trains from the City right through to Chesham in the peak hour). As for the going underfoot it is reasonable at all times save for the short stretch of Pump Lane, the possible problems being alluded to in the itinerary.

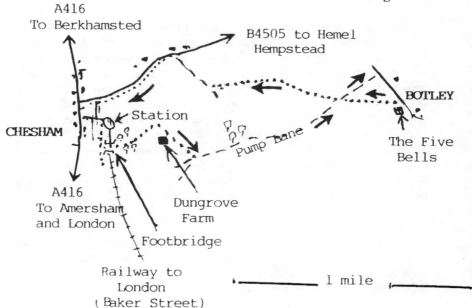

A416
To Berkhamsted

B4505 to Hemel
Hempstead

BOTLEY

Station

CHESHAM

The Five
Bells

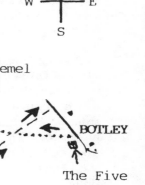

Pump Lane

A416
To Amersham
and London

Dungrove
Farm

Footbridge

Railway to
London
(Baker Street)

1 mile

CHESHAM lies in a hollow around the headwaters of the River Chess. The latter rises close to the town centre. Just below there are extensive watercress beds, the quality of the water being conducive to growth of this product. The High Street forms the spine of the town and all turnings off quickly rise into the surrounding hills. In some respects the locality can be described as being the heart of the Chiltern Hills. In the 19th century the ever enterprising Metropolitan Railway linked Chesham to London by a 3 mile long branch line from Chalfont and Latimer (formerly Chalfont Road) station. This little single line backwater has survived the Beeching Era. The shuttle train still wends its way around a series of reverse curves as it descends from the heights of Chalfont to the valley bottom at Chesham.

Leaving Chesham station by the one and only exit, turn to your left and follow an alley which runs parallel to the line. You soon reach a footbridge on your left. Cross this and follow a clear path which soon assumes a steeply uphill course through wooded ground. At the head of this climb you cross two stiles in quick succession. Then keep a forward course over the field. After crossing a third stile go left along a clear path which follows the left hand edge of the field. Crossing yet another stile turn to your right along an old driveway. Where this goes right into the vicinity of the farm, cross a double stile and keep forward to cross a further stile which adjoins an iron gate. With the hedge and the farm buildings on the right, you descend slightly and at the valley bottom you join . . .

PUMP LANE, a hereabouts sunken trackway that has come up from the valley *en route* for the higher ground. In its lower reaches the lane has become 'suburbanised' but, at the point where the ramble joins it, nothing but pure rurality prevail.

On entering Pump Lane turn to the left. At this point it should be mentioned that hereabouts the surface of the lane can sometimes resemble that of a partly dried-up duck pond. If these conditions prevail it seems permissive to walk parallel to the lane just inside the hedge. Whether you are in the lane or the field the choice no longer becomes available at a point a little way on, where you encounter some wooded ground. By this point the surface of the lane becomes passable at all times and should be followed for some 1½ miles until it ends upon meeting a tiny surfaced by-road. On the way and as you gradually gain height, ignore footpaths which deviate to your right and left. On reaching the T-junction with the small road, turn right and still gaining in height you soon reach on your right . . .

THE FIVE BELLS. A rural tavern down this narrow road which virtually leads to nowhere. It lies some half mile south of a hamlet known as Botley. The beer garden is in pretty surroundings and the interior is delightful. A tempting selection of cask beers are available, with an equally wide choice of snacks. At the time of research for this volume it should be noted that food is not available at Sunday lunchtimes (unusual to find this in the Chiltern area). When you can take the decision to leave this delightful inn.

The Five Bells, Botley Walk.

Cross a stile to the right of the pub's front and follow a clear path ahead. In less than a quarter of a mile you come to a junction of paths. Here turn rightwards dropping quite steeply downhill to cross Pump Lane which you will recall from the outward route.

Having crossed the lane the ensuing path ascends to a stile after which it follows the same course through the next field, eventually arriving at the right hand hedge. Follow the boundary for a short half mile and you emerge into a neat farm drive which follow to your right. Soon the drive emerges into a 'B' road. Go left here. The left hand pavement soon parts company from the road itself, the latter descending rapidly. Eventually the path itself descends (even more rapidly) and having come to a junction of roads go left and ahead back to Chesham station.

Vintage signal cabin at Chesham.

Walk 7

GREAT MISSENDEN to 'the Full Moon', LITTLE KINGSHILL, and back

BY RAIL . . . Chiltern Line trains from London (Marylebone), service interval ½ hourly weekdays and Saturday. Very sparse on Sundays*, when you are recommended to take London Underground (Metropolitan) line from Baker Street, changing into a shuttle (hourly) service at Amersham.

BY ROAD . . . From London area, A40 to a point beyond junction 1 of M40. Thereafter follow A413 via Amersham By-pass to a point just before Great Missenden, where follow sign to village. Station is on your left at end of High Street. From a northerly aspect join M25 and drive anti-clockwise to junction 18, then westwards on A404 to Amersham By-pass, thence by A413 as above.

MAP . . . Ordnance Survey Landranger Sheet or Explorer Sheets 2 and 3.

DISTANCE OF WALK . . . Approximately 5½ miles.

TOPOGRAPHY . . . Up in the hills to the south of the valley of the tiny Misbourne River lies high ground, with remote villages. The prospect around shows extensive beech woods, many of which used for the furniture factories at High Wycombe. There is no 'blot' on the landscape to behold. The industries of the valley of the River Wye are some 350 feet below and not visible from the hilltops. The ascent soon after the start of the walk is gentle, and mainly involves a narrow farm lane, which after servicing the farm itself peters out into a delightful mainly hedged right of way. The going in the latter can be sticky after rainfall, but otherwise the well signposted paths are easily negotiated at all seasons.

* *Improvememnts promised for 1998.*

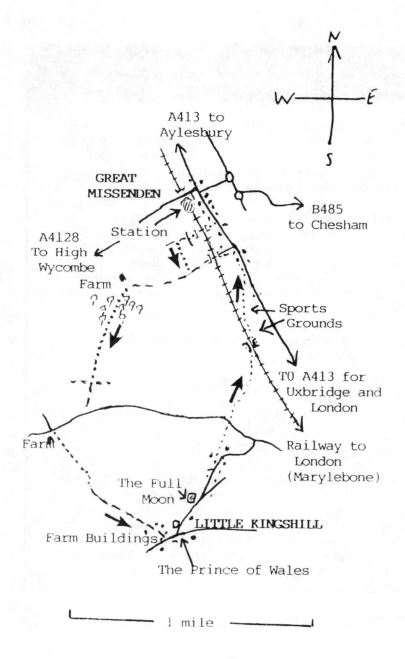

N

W — E

S

A413 to
Aylesbury

**GREAT
MISSENDEN**

A4128
To High
Wycombe

Station

B485
to Chesham

Farm

Sports
Grounds

TO A413 for
Uxbridge and
London

Farm

Railway to
London
(Marylebone)

The Full
Moon

LITTLE KINGSHILL

Farm Buildings

The Prince of Wales

1 mile

52

GREAT MISSENDEN is a fairly large village, the character of which has not changed very much in a lifetime. It lies in the upper valley of the Misbourne River, a stream that sometimes flourishes and sometimes dries up altogether for years on end. The narrow and picturesque main street retains much of its quietude on account of a by-pass road that cuts into the side of the valley on the northern side. The parish church is situated in an otherwise isolated position on the hillside to the north-east and is reached by a blind lane that crosses the by-pass road by a modern bridge. The modern church at the crossroads near the station is for the Roman Catholic community. There is a strong Polish element in the parish following 'resettlement' during and after World War 2. Some 2½ miles north-west of the village is Dutchlands Summit, the highest point of the London to Aylesbury road and railway during their traverse of The Chiltern Hills.

Leaving the station by the main exit on the 'up' side, descend and at the cross roads turn right in to the High Street. Just before passing The George Hotel go right along a narrow alley. Cross a 'back road' by turning left for a few yards and then right into an unmade road. At its end go forward and under a railway arch. Emerging into a gravelly road ahead turn right and then in about 30 yards left along a grassy track. Ahead is a stile and gate. Do not cross either but instead turn left along a little enclosed path which leads out into a tarred lane, where turn right.

Follow this narrow road, eventually passing a farm on your right. At this point the road becomes a track, which follow through a wooded dip and on to join a metalled farm drive. Here go ahead (slightly rightwards). On joining a secondary road bear right. The road rises and in some 200 yards at a T-junction there is on your left a farm entrance. Go towards the entrance but not through it. Instead cross a stile on your left. The clear path runs ahead, firstly with a hedge on the right and then across the middle of this large field. Ignoring a path on the right the way lies ahead leaving the field via a stile. Having crossed the stile keep right for a few yards through a gap into an orchard and on to a track with the orchard on your right. Follow the track, eventually passing between farm buildings and out into a little road at . . .

LITTLE KINGSHILL, a hilltop village, remote from civilisation as we know it. It is typical of the many hilltop 'settlements' that abound in the 'High Chilterns' . . . just a scattering of homesteads and a couple of pleasant pubs, and a meeting place of by-roads.

On approaching the road, turn to your left. Passing (or visiting?) The Prince of Wales, take the left hand fork at the junction of minor roads. On your left you soon come to . . .

THE FULL MOON, with its large and attractive south facing garden and its pleasant exterior. Inside, the accommodation is extensive and in addition to good food and/or snacks, there is a wide variety of cask beers. In typically mid-Chiltern surroundings, The Full Moon is a place to linger and to enjoy the clean air and tranquil surroundings.

Leaving the inn, follow on down the lane to a point where on your left a private road forks off, New Road which follow. Where there is a turning on your left called Wychwood, ignore this and instead go slightly leftwards along a little enclosed alley which descends quite steeply and crosses another residential road. Soon after this the alley emerges into a field via a stile. Ignoring a stile away on your right, which oddly enough leads into someone's private back garden, the path continues diagonally over the field, passing the corner of house gardens, at which point it veers slightly more rightwards to another stile some 35 yards ahead. In the next field the path moves in a rightwards direction into a dip adjacent to an electricity pole.

About 40 yards on, cross a stile on your right and go under a little tunnel-like bridge under the railway line. On emerging, you enter a large sports ground. Go diagonally left across this (circumnavigating it if games are in progress) to the far corner. Here you join the main road, where keep forward for a short way and so into Great Missenden High Street and at its far end, turning left to the railway station.

Walk 8

STOKE MANDEVILLE to 'the Prince of Wales', MARSH, and back

BY RAIL . . . Chiltern Railways from London (Marylebone) via Harrow-on-the-Hill, Rickmansworth, Amersham, etc. Service twice hourly weekdays and Saturdays. On Sundays, use London (Baker Street) to Amersham, changing for 'shuttle' service on to Stoke Mandeville (hourly)*.

BY ROAD . . . From London area via A40 to Denham, thence A413 through Amersham. Some 3 miles short of Aylesbury, turn left along A4010 for short half mile to Stoke Mandeville station. From a northerly direction aim for Luton and Dunstable, leaving M1 at junction 11 between these two towns. From Dunstable take A5 northwards, and after some 2 miles turn left on to A505 and thence its continuation, A418 towards Aylesbury. Thereafter A413 for some 3 miles where turn right on A4010 for Stoke Mandeville. Station and car park are on left before crossing railway bridge.

MAP . . . Ordnance Survey Landranger Sheet 165 or Explorer Sheet 2.

DISTANCE OF WALK . . . Approximately 5½miles.

TOPOGRAPHY . . . Rambles in Bucks. frequently encounter the great Vale of Aylesbury. This tract of land is not entirely flat. Unlike Eastern England's Fenlands there are little ups and downs and indeed some villages set upon hilltops. The great pastures and ample hedgerows make for a really rural ramble. Away from the county town of Aylesbury lies a labarynth of public rights of way across the peaceful countryside. In recent years they have been well waymarked and signposted, but in Autumn when the fields have been newly harrowed the actual course of some of the paths might be indistinct. If your enjoy crossing stiles this is the walk for you. They are so ubiquitious that the author nearly forgot how many he had crossed before arriving at The Prince of Wales pub! As for the going, sufficient be it to say that appropriate footwear should be worn at all times, save for periods following a prolonged spell of dry weather.

* *Some trains now run direct from Marylebone on Sundays. Service is infrequent. Improvements promised 1998.*

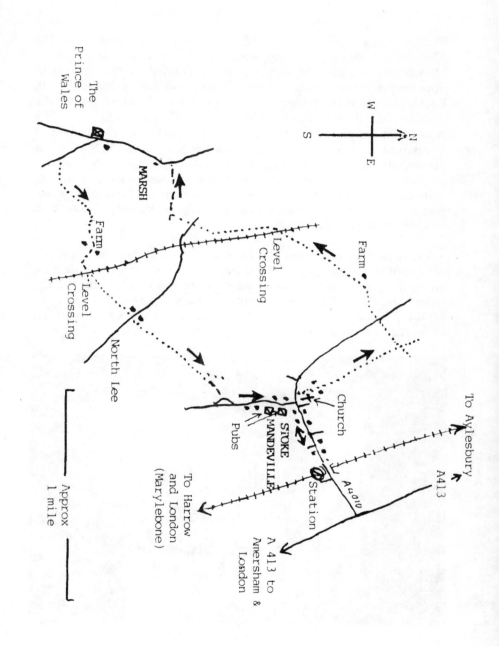

The Prince of Wales

MARSH

Farm

Level Crossing

Level Crossing

North Lee

Farm

Level Crossing

Pubs

STOKE MANDEVILLE

Church

Station

A 4010

To Harrow and London (Marylebone)

A 413 to Amersham & London

To Aylesbury

A413

Approx 1 mile

N
W   E
S

STOKE MANDEVILLE, as we find it today, is a product of The Metropolitan Railway, which was originally planned to run from Manchester to Paris (through a Channel Tunnel). In the fullness of time the project extended only from Verney Junction in deepest North Buckinghamshire to New Cross in South East London! Before the railway arrived, Stoke Mandeville was a tiny sleepy village with a few cottages, a couple of pubs and a parish church, etc. The ribbon of development between the station and the old village testifies to its present status of a not unattractive outpost of the commuter belt . . . an oasis in the sleepy vale of Aylesbury . . . a nice place to return to after a day in the turmoil of The City. The famous hospital is some way to the north of the village, almost within the bounds of extended, built-up modern Aylesbury.

Leave the station by the main exit and at the end of the approach road turn left across the line and proceed ahead for some half mile along the main road. At an intersection of busy roads you see the church on your right. Immediately after passing the church, go right across a stile on to an enclosed path which runs between outbuildings and then crosses a small floodlight-equipped

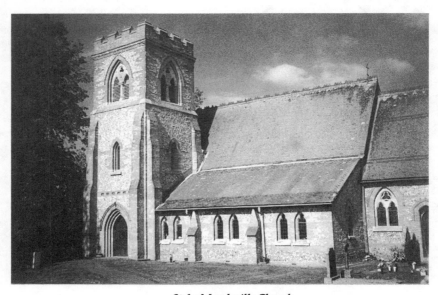

Stoke Mandeville Church.

equestrian ring. Leaving the ring via a stile, the way lies forward across a field to another stile, after which the clear path runs along the left hand side of the next field, (the low buildings of the hospital can be seen ahead). In the middle of the field you come to a 'crossroads' of paths. Here turn sharply left across a metal stile and on, with the hedge on your left, to another similarly constructed stile which cross to emerge in a busy main road.

Cross the road (with due care) to path opposite, which runs for a short way with a high hedge on the left. Where the hedge bends off to your left, take a course a little to your right; the path (which at certain times of the year may be indistinct) aims for the far right corner of the field where you will find a stile, which cross. Immediately ahead is another stile. Do not cross this but instead keep more or less forward through a paddock, with the fencing on your right. Cross two more stiles (in close succession) and keep forward with the boundary of the field on your left, descending very slightly to cross a brook. Ahead is another stile leading into a large field. On the stile is a waymark. If you follow the direction of this across the field you will in some quarter mile come to a further stile, beyond which is a railway line.

Cross the track, being sure to heed the 'stop, look and listen' sign, remembering that this railway is single track and a train might be approaching from either direction. Having made your way over the rails, turn left for a few paces and then go right over another stile. Then turn left parallel to the railway, coming after a short while to a little wooded area (with more stiles to cross within). Leaving the wood and passing under electricity wires, go to your right across another stile over a fence and then keep forward to emerge in a minor road (via yet another stile!). Cross the road to a path opposite, entry into which is by a swing gate (such a change after all those stiles) and forward through two more swing gates, emerging into a green track, where turn right. The track leads after some quarter mile into another minor road.

Turn to your left at this road which bends to the right and then to the left. You are currently in . . .

MARSH, not really a village or even a hamlet, but better described as a 'place on the map', consisting as it does of isolated homesteads, a farm, the aforementioned road junction and . . .

Continuing along the road for a short half mile you come to . . .

THE PRINCE OF WALES, a partly thatched building with the sign outside indicating that 'ABC' (Aylesbury Brewery Company) supply the victuals. The brewery at Aylesbury has long been closed but ABC bitter is still available within and very palatable stuff it is too. This isolated inn exudes within a cordial atmosphere and the landlord proclaimed that he himself goes rambling around the neighbourhood. 'Pub Grub' is not available here, so be prepared to feast on potato crisps, nuts, etc. They still go down very well with a glass of cask ale! There is a spacious beer garden at the back, and there is a 'beer table' across the way on the greensward at the road junction.

Leave The Prince of Wales via the road opposite. After some 500 yards turn left on to a clear path which pursues a course along the right hand side of a large field. On reaching the far right hand corner of this field, go to your right for a few yards, and where the hedge bends sharply to the left, go left but instead of keeping to the hedge follow the course of the path diagonally over the field to the entrance of a farm and its outbuildings. As you pass between the buildings, look out for a public footpath sign on your right.

Beer tables on the green.

Entering by crossing a stile, go forward across two more stiles, one each side of the railway track (once again crossing the line with utmost care).

Beyond the railway crossing you traverse a narrow field and another stile, over which is a sign indicating a junction of paths. Take the left hand branch and follow the path which runs accompanied by electricity poles and wires, and after slightly rising joins a minor road with a bungalow on your left. This is . . .

NORTH LEE, which like Marsh is more of a name on a map than a hamlet. A few houses and bungalows straddle the lane through North Lee . . . it is an area which exudes isolation, yet it is so near to the bustling county town of Aylesbury. The ground rises slightly hereabouts, belying the claim that the great vale is entirely flat.

Cross the road and go right for a few paces, then turn left along a clear path which ascends slightly with the grounds of a house on your left. After about 40 yards look for a stile on your left through the hedge. Keep forward here (the path has merely passed from one side of the hedge to the other) and having crossed a stile into the next field you come at the end of that field, and just to your left a little unmade lane. Turn right and follow this lane, which soon leads out into a 'spur' of a main road. Turn left here and follow to the junction of roads by Stoke Mandeville church, passing (or pausing) at, on your right, a couple of inns, The Woolpack (and?) or The Bull. At the junction by the church, the route concludes with the short trek back to Stoke Mandeville station.

Walk 9

WENDOVER to 'the Russell Arms', BUTLERS CROSS (Edlesborough), and back

BY RAIL . . . Wendover Station is on the Marylebone to Aylesbury arm of the Chiltern Line. A half-hourly service operates on weekdays and on Sundays the service is hourly. The Sunday service starts from Baker Street station in London, with a change of trains at Amersham*.

BY ROAD . . . A40 (Western Avenue) from London. At Denham roundabout, follow A40 (not M40) to junction with A413 at Tatling End. Follow A413 through The Chalfonts and Amersham through to Wendover. Turn left at T-junction in town. A few yards to the right by the Shoulder of Mutton pub go right into station car park. From the north, leave M25 at junction 11 through Dunstable, thence B489 to Ivinghoe, after which via B488 to join A41 at top of Tring Hill, which descend turning left on to B4011 into Wendover.

MAP . . . Ordnance Survey Landranger Sheet 165 or Explorer Sheet 2.

DISTANCE OF WALK . . . Approximately 4 miles.

TOPOGRAPHY . . . This is a ramble of great contrasts. It begins with an ascent to one of the highest points in The Chilterns, a rapid descent to a really countrified pub, followed as a complete contrast by a leisurely return to Wendover across a corner of The Vale of Aylesbury. There is no need to be daunted by the initial climb. Although a mile or so long, the ascent is in the main gradual. Indeed it is significant to note that the inhabitants of Wendover, including those of pensionable age, make it the venue for their Sunday afternoon stroll. The descent via an old sunken trackway needs care as there are loose stones underfoot. The ascent of Coombe Hill has its just reward in a great vista to the north as you gain height. You may find space at a premium on the bench seat just below the summit, but if you are lucky it is a place to relax and linger.

An infrequent service now operates from Marylebone to Amersham on Sundays. More improvements promised for 1998.

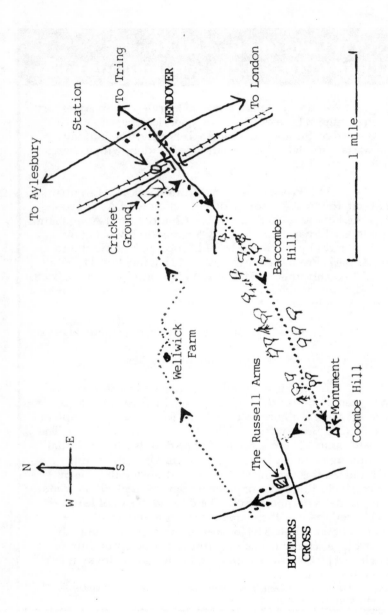

WENDOVER is still today a largely unspoilt country town, nestling below the 800 feet high escarpment of The Chiltern Hills. The high ground hereabouts gives way to the north west to the flatter, but undulating, pastures of the great Vale of Aylesbury. The town centre abounds with pleasant inns and eating places. At one time Wendover had its connection to the inland waterway system, via the Wendover Arm, a now derelict canal that linked up with the mighty Grand Union a few miles away at Marsworth. The picturesque wharf which lay on the edge of the town is now no more, its place having been taken by residential development.

Leave Wendover station by the approach road, at the top of which, cross (by turning right) the railway line and a newly constructed by-pass road. The road rises rapidly with cottages on your right, and soon bends quite sharply to the right. Here go forward and left to a choice of footpaths and take the right hand fork of the two, ignoring a further fork to the right in a few more yards. The track continues to ascend, shortly giving the choice of following an old sunken way or some recently constructed steps to the right hand side thereof. As you gain height, you eventually (after some half mile) reach a grassy area. Take the right hand side gate, after which the pathway rises rapidly through the wooded ground. You eventually cross an old sunken lane and, having crossed this, a patch of greensward ahead leads to the summit of . . .

COOMBE HILL some 800 feet above sea level, and crowned with an obelisk, commemorating those who fell in the South African Wars. This is one of the classic viewpoints of the Home Counties. On a clear day, one can see northwards as far as the 'wold' country which lies beyond the town of Northampton. You are gazing over the 'great divide' between the chalk hills of South East England to the seemingly endless Midland Plains.

Return from the obelisk to the sunken lane and here go left following this ancient trackway, descending rapidly to join a road by Edlesborough Golf Club. Turn left along the road, which (still descending) arrives in a short quarter of a mile at . . .

Coombe Hill with its obelisk.

The summit, Coombe Hill.

BUTLERS CROSS, a meeting place of roads of ancient origin. The road from which you emerge is the prehistoric Icknield Way. Butlers Cross is in the parish of Edlesborough, which within its bounds lies Chequers, the country retreat of prime ministers.

Turn right at the cross roads and on your immediate right is ...

THE RUSSELL ARMS, a lovely old pub with saloon and public bars and with beer tables at the west-facing frontage. Amongst the limited range of cask ales is the 'resurrected' ABC Best Bitter, which in years gone by used to be brewed locally at nearby Aylesbury. The food menu is comprehensive and is varied at weekends. If you happen to order a portion of chips with your meal, prepare to devour an enormous helping, so deliciously fried that they would please the palate of a discerning visitor from the North of England! Such a change from the soggy mess that appears so often to be the characteristic of southern suburban takeaways!

Leave the Russell Arms and turn to your right. In some 300 yards lies a footpath (entitled 'The Aylesbury Ring') on your right and follow this up rising ground to a stile after which the way is at the

A doggy flap in a stile.

right hand margin of a large field. (Note the unusual feature of 'dog flaps' at the stiles hereabouts.) At the third and fourth fields the path runs through their respective middles, eventually arriving via another stile into an area with a few trees on your right. Leaving this area go forward with the boundary of farm buildings on your right and where the boundary goes off at a right angle go half right through a dip to a stile and iron gate some 40 yards ahead. This is ...

WELWICK FARM, which at one time was the home of the strict Judge Jeffries (known for his severity as the 'hanging judge'). The farmhouse and its surroundings were a peaceful place to return in the evenings, after a day at the assizes, committing villains to return to their maker!

After passing the gate and stile cross the farm road and then veer to the left and after a few yards to the right. The path continues with a field boundary on your right. After crossing a stile, go sharp left. The path continues veering slightly away from the wire fencing on your left to a stile some 15 yards from the left hand corner of the field. Having crossed this stile take the right hand branch of two paths, going diagonally across the field to eventually reach a cricket ground on your left. Passing the playing field, you join a lane which soon leads out into the road, where turn left over the bridge across the by-pass and railway, and left into station yard.

Walk 10

GORING AND STREATLEY STATION (Goring-on-Thames) to 'the White Lion', CRAYS POND, and back

BY RAIL . . . Thames Trains from London (Paddington), sometimes, particularly on Sundays, a change is required at Reading. Service ½ hourly, hourly at weekends.

BY ROAD . . . From London area, M40 to junction 12, thence A40 for 1 mile into Theale village, where turn right on to A340. At Pangbourne village join A229. Four miles on, at Streatley, turn right on to B4526 over river into Goring-on-Thames. Station and car park are on your right at far end of village. From a northerly aspect join M25 and proceed anti-clockwise to junction 15, thence M40 as above. Alternatively from north a more rural route, by leaving M1 at junction 11 (between Luton and Dunstable), thence through Dunstable town on to B489 to Ivinghoe, B485 to join A41. After a mile leave the latter via B4544, then right for a mile on joining A413, then left on to B4009 all the way to Goring-on-Thames.

MAP . . . Ordnance Survey Pathfinder Sheet 175 or Explorer Sheet 3.

DISTANCE OF WALK . . . Approximately 6 miles.

TOPOGRAPHY . . . If you like hilly and/or wooded country, then this is the walk for you. If you also like bluebells go in late April or early May. This is a lovely corner of South-East England, where one ridge of chalk hills are separated from the other by The Thames Valley. On the 'outward' route, there is only one really steep pitch, this falling within the first mile. Otherwise the climb to Crays Pond is long but gentle. Returning after the visit to The White Lion, the gradient is almost 90% in the walker's favour. The paths in the main are in reasonable condition all the year round, as the chalky subsoil is porous and water soon seeps through. The only exception is where the bridleway runs through the valley on the outgoing walk. This can become 'puddly' in the wake of horse traffic.

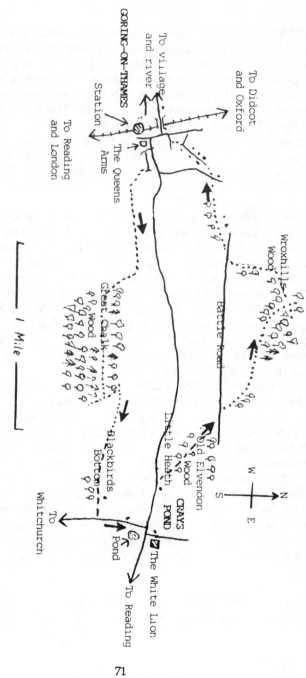

GORING-ON-THAMES

To Didcot
and Oxford

To village
and river

Station

The Queens
Arms

To Reading
and London

Wroxhills
Wood

Battle Road

Great Chalk
Wood

Blackbirds
Bottom

Little Heath

Old Elvendon
Wood

N
W — E
S

CRAYS
POND

Pond

The White Lion

To
Whitchurch

To Reading

1 Mile

71

GORING-ON-THAMES is one of the most attractive villages on the river, situated as it is within a narrow valley between The Oxfordshire Chilterns and The Berkshire Downs. It is 'twinned' with Streatley village on the opposite (Berkshire) bank, the parishes being linked by a somewhat ordinary bridge, which however commands spectacular views of the neighbouring lock and weir. The surrounding hills are well wooded and on the Berkshire side very steep sided. To geographers the area is knows as the 'Goring Gap'. Within Goring village there are four really delightful country inns, the predominating brews being local (Oxfordshire) ales from Morrells of Oxford, Brakspear of Henley-on-Thames or Morland of Abingdon.

Leave the station by the main exit on the 'up' (east) side and turn left in the yard. In a few yards turn right with The Queens Arms pub on the corner. Thereafter take a right turn into a residential road, Whitehills Green. In a few yards turn left between modern houses and at the end of this road take a right hand turn into a 'dead end' that ensues. Here a little passageway goes forward between house gardens, soon emerging into a field via a stile. Go half left across the field to the remains of a stile or gate in the corner. The way then veers left and follows quite steeply uphill with the hedge on your left. To the rear is a great vista of the 'Goring Gap' with The Berkshire Downs as a backdrop.

The path eventually eaches the corner of a field and goes rightwards with a hedge still on the left, and descends very steeply into a dry valley. Cross a stile into the corner of some downland and in a few yards another into Great Chalk Wood. The tiny, but clear, path begins to ascend from the valley bottom, and shortly assumes that character of a forest track. In a full mile (after still gradually ascending) the track descends for a few yards to join another path leading in from your right. Here turn sharply left. In a few yards you are back in the valley bottom, where go right into a bridleway that is gradually climbing the valley. The way becomes enclosed for a short way in the vicinity of a line dwelling house, after which the route becomes a gravelly drive. The locality hereabouts is known as . . .

BLACKBIRD'S BOTTTOM, a really peaceful spot which because of its situation amongst the surrounding hills remains isolated from the sounds of modern life. It is really a delightful place to linger for a while before completing the ascent of the hill tops.

In the vicinity of further dwellings, the drive becomes tarred and soon you will hear the passing traffic on the B471 road, which upon joining you turn to the left. In a quarter mile you come to an intersection of roads at . . .

CRAYS POND, not so much a village as a 'locality', consisting as it does of the road junction, the pond, a garage, a scattering of houses and the pub. It is an airy spot, situated as it is some 650 feet above sea level. The pond itself is encountered on your right just before the intersection of roads. It is partly overgrown with reeds but is

Pond and pump, Crays Pond.

nevertheless delightful to behold. The greensward between the road and the water has been landscaped with a seat to rest on, and in the fore-ground is the original village pump. Ahead and across the road is . . .

THE WHITE LION, a lovely inn with a capacious south-western facing beer garden. The interior has a rural and unspoiled character. Beers from Morland of Abingdon are available including the 'premium' ale, 'Old Speckled Hen'. There is a comprehensive selection of snacks and meals to suit all diets and tastes.

Leaving the pub cross the road and take the route signposted to Goring and Streatley. After some quarter of a mile, go to the right along a rough track, with a sign indicating that you are approaching . . .

LITTLE HEATH, an 'outpost' of Crays pond with a few houses. There are many places of the same name throughout the British Isles. Little Heath may vie with the Whitchurches or the Newtowns as the nation's most ubiquitious place name.

The track soon enters Wroxhill Wood and goes steeply downhill, eventually joining a small road in the valley (Battle Road), where bear left. In a few yards leave the road via a path on your right, which leaves the valley bottom and continues ahead, eventually running between a fence on the left and wooded ground on the right. The path soon enters the wood and veers gradually rightwards. In the middle of the wood you come to a crossing path. Here turn sharp left. The path soon begins to descend to the perimeter of the woods, where it continues leftwards and ahead, with fencing on the right, eventually emerging back in Battle Road, which cross to a designated 'cycleway'. The enclosed path eventually crosses a stile and leads slightly leftwards in a field to another stile and out into a road. (Pity the poor cyclists who have to negotiate the stiles with their machines.) Cross this road to the greensward opposite and on to a paved path where bear left. The path soon leads out into the end of a residential road, which follow downhill till a point where it bends to the right. At this point go forward along an alley, soon joining a little road where bear left to soon join a busy road where turn left for The Queens Arms and the railway station.

Thames train departing from Goring and Steatley.

FOR THOSE WISHING TO VISIT THE VILLAGE CENTRE . . .
Cross the station via the footbridge and leave the platform on the
'down' side. Follow a narrow road which passes The Catherine Wheel
pub on your right. The lane soon veers right with The John Barleycorn
pub also on your right. At a T-junction ahead turn left for the bridge
and the river.

Walk 11

CHOLSEY to 'the Chequers', ASTON TIRROLD, and back

BY RAIL . . . Cholsey is served by stopping trains from Reading to Oxford. From London (Paddington) it usually involves a change at Reading.

BY ROAD . . . As for Walk 10, but at Streatley pass through village to fork junction and continue for 3 miles, where take a left hand turn on unclassified road into Cholsey. If taking alternative from northerly aspect, leave B4009 on to Wallingford By-pass, thence right on to A329. Take unclassified road on right to Cholsey village.

MAP . . . Ordnance Survey Pathfinder Sheet 174.

DISTANCE OF WALK . . . Approximately 5¼ miles.

TOPOGRAPHY . . . West of where the Chiltern Hills are bounded by The Thames, lies the locality of South Oxfordshire, mainly an expanse of flatter gound. This is known as The Vale of White Horse, on account of an equine carving on the hills above Uffington some 12 miles westward. To the south the vale is bounded by the rolling heights of the Berkshire Downs. Hereabouts the vale itself abounds in little hillocks, amongst which are The Sinodum Hills and the rising ground beyond Aston Tirrold village. The only 'blot' on the landscape are the cooling towers of Didcot power station. When these were erected there was rightly much brouhaha about desecration of the landscape, but erected they duly were! This is a very level ramble, the only real rise and fall being the ramps to and from the bridge over the main railway line. The surrounding hills always provide an interesting backdrop. Underfoot the going is reasonable, apart from the possibilities of 'soft patches' in the bridleway on the return journey, but even these can be by-passed with the minimum of ingenuity.

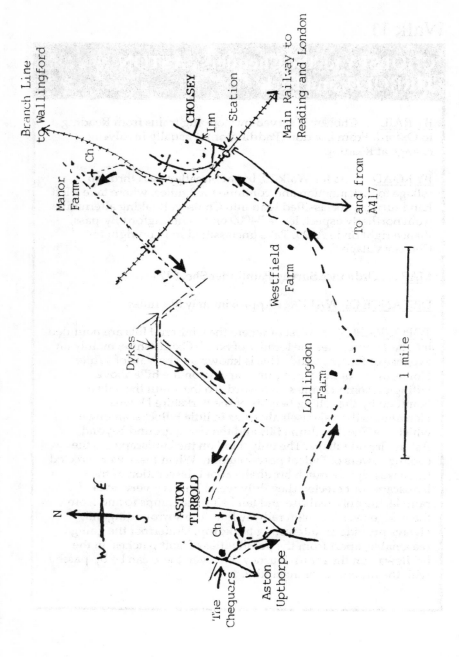

CHOLSEY is a quiet village at the foot of The Berkshire Downs. Before boundary changes took place, the locality was in Berkshire, but like the neighbouring market town of Wallingford it is now within South Oxfordshire. Being as it is on the main railway line, Cholsey has tended to 'develop'. There are fast and frequent commuter services to Reading and London. New habitation is entirely confined to the northern side of the railway, the other side remaining pastoral with isolated farmhouses. The station was formerly known as Cholsey and Moulsford, the latter being some two miles to the south and containing within its purlieus one fo the most renowned of Thames-side hotels, the 'Beetle and Wedge', with opulent grounds running down to the river's edge. Cholsey station is now again a junction for a branch line to Wallingford. Enthusiasts operate a limited vintage and/or steam train between Cholsey and Wallingford.

Leaving the station go left along an alley which soon emerges into a residential road. After a point where the road has veered to the right, and opposite a turning called Sandy Lane, go left along an enclosed path. *After* passing under an arch, bear right through the remains of an old kissing gate. The path continues ahead over a stile and a wooden bridge (with the railway line on your right). Having crossed two more stiles in close succession, the path goes left and diagonally towards yet another stile which leads into a churchyard. Go forwards towards the church door and then turn left, passing the church on your right and leaving the graveyard via a stile near its far corner. Then follow a path which shortly emerges into a farm road, where turn left. Having crossed a bridge over the main Great Western railway line, the farm road goes right, towards some buildings. Ignoring the right turn keep straight ahead with some wooded ground on your right. Soon you cross a substantial bridge over an equally substantial dyke.

Here, turn to the right with the dyke on your right. In some quarter of a mile the path veers leftwards with a lesser dyke now on your right. Ignoring a concrete bridge go straight on under electric wires. The dyke on your right eventually peters out, giving way to a wire fence and, arriving at a junction of paths, turn to your right with a small river on your left. Look northwards here (to your right) and you will see . . .

THE SINODUN HILLS, each of the two peaks crowned with groups of trees known as THE WITTENHAM CLUMPS. An ancient British camp lay on the foothills. Slightly to the right is an isolated hummock, BRITWELL BARROW which appears to be topped by a single tree! Behind these isolated uplands lies The Thames and the delightful village of Little Wittenham, with neighbouring Day's Lock one of the most peaceful stretches of the whole river.

Continuing with the stream on your left, the path eventually becomes 'concreted' and having passed an iron gate the concrete section turns abruptly to the right. Ignoring the right turn, the path keeps straight ahead over a stile and along a 'green way' and out into a by-road on the fringe of . . .

ASTON TIRROLD which is 'twinned' with Aston Upthorpe (where one ends and the other begins is difficult to discern), two sleepy villages at the foot of the downs. The minor roads that peregrinate amid the cottages bear little traffic – hereabouts it is as if it is always Sunday! The locality is a gathering ground of streams which flow merrily to and fro, sometimes behind hedges, some in roadside

The church at Cholsey.

ditches, and others spilling their contents over the highways after spells of wet weather. To the west of the Astons lies a small undulation, Blewburton Hill, behind which is a further expanse of the great Vale of White Horse. The horse itself lies some miles away to the west.

Turn left at the road and continue to a point where there is a church on your right. Take a path through the churchyard and a little beyond to another minor road, where turn right. You soon emerge at . . .

THE CHEQUERS, situated at the junction of 'village lanes'. Conversation in the bar frequently centres on the subject of '10 to 1 winners' and of horses 'still running', for this is racing country and a glance at the Ordnance Survey map will show many 'gallops' on the hills southwards of the village. The deletion of the name of one of the national breweries is prominent on the inn sign, indicating that the establishment is now a free house. Fullers London Pride, Marstons Pedigree, and Morlands' Old Speckled Hen are apparently available at most times, with the addition of a guest beer. An omnibus stop sign can be seen across the road, but lest any reader contemplates

curtailing the walk by resorting to public transport, let he or she be warned. The adjacent timetable indicates that there is one bus a week – on Tuesdays only!

Leaving The Chequers, retrace your steps, ignoring that path that leads from the church, continuing on to a junction of two roads, Aston Street and Baker Street. A few yards past the junction, go left along a bridleway. After about a mile this ancient track becomes tarred in the neighbourhood of a farm. Where the tarred section eventually turns right proceed straight on. Soon the track becomes 'surfaced' again in the vicinity of another farm. Just after this farm drive has turned sharply to the right, take a track on your left, soon passing under a railway arch and rejoining the outgoing route. Turn right along the residential road and then the short alley to Cholsey station.

Walk 12

SHIPLAKE STATION (Lower Shiplake) to 'the White Hart', SHIPLAKE ROW and back

BY RAIL . . . Hourly service from London (Paddington), changing for Shiplake at Twyford. Similar arrangement from westward direction from Reading and beyond.

BY ROAD . . . From London area, M4 to junction 7 where follow signs to and through Maidenhead (A4). Continue on A4 for some 12 miles, then turn right along B476 crossing Thames at Sonning. Reaching A4155 turn right for some 3 miles through Shiplake old village and beyond, taking a right-hand turn along Station Road to Shiplake Station. From a more northerly aspect, leave M25 at Junction 16, thence M40 westward to junction 3. Thereafter A4094 for approximately 2 miles to Bourne End, then A4155 through Marlow and Henley-on-Thames. Station Road, Shiplake is on right some 2 miles beyond Henley.

MAP . . . Ordnance Survey Landranger Sheet 175.

DISTANCE . . . Approximately 5 miles.

TOPOGRAPHY . . . The area traversed is a gentle slope where the South Oxfordshire Chilterns meet the Thames Valley. On the outward route you will be gradually gaining height until the 300 feet contour is reached at Binfield Heath. The journey thereafter is all flat or on the downgrade. This extreme southerly corner of Oxfordshire is well wooded and mainly unspoiled. The footpaths are clear and comparatively well used. After a rainy spell, the woodland and the riverside path can be decidedly sticky.

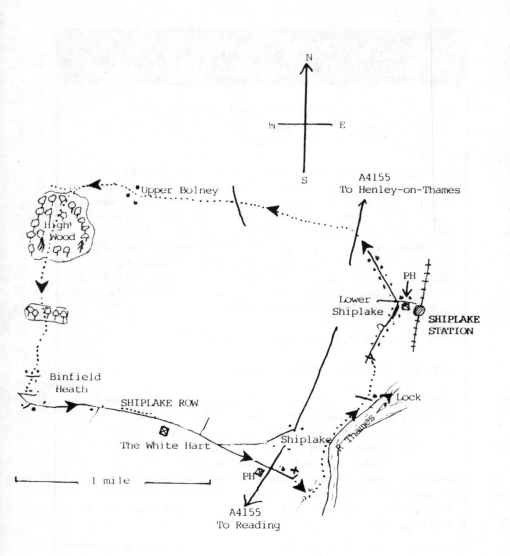

SHIPLAKE STATION is in a locality known as LOWER SHIPLAKE. Shiplake village itself is some one mile away to the south-west. Lower Shiplake is the product of Brunel's Great Western Railway. In the early days of this project a branch line was built from the main line at Twyford through Shiplake to Henley-on-Thames. The surroundings in the neighbourhood of the station are mainly of opulent properties. Obviously a 'dormitory' for those whose daily pilgrimages to the City of London has, through the medium of their labours, brought them an above average measure of prosperity. The 'epicentre' of Lower Shiplake is adjacent to the railway level crossing, consisting of a general store with the highly appropriate name of The Corner Shop, across the road from which is a modernish public house, The Baskerville Arms.

Leave the station without crossing the line and pass the pub on your left and the shop on your right. Here take a right-hand turning, Northfield Avenue, which follow to its end some half mile on. The way continues in a forward direction in th form of a path enclosed between wooden fences, emerging in some 100 yards into the main Reading—Henley road. Cross this busy highway (with great care) and go forward by way of a rough lane which soon begins to rise under an umbrella of trees. This lane eventually meets a small public road, which cross to continue along a private drive which is also a public right of way and a bridleway.

After something in excess of half a mile the drive bends right and then to the left amidst an assortment of isolated dwellings, some old and some modern. This 'backwater' of habitation is apparently known as Upper Bolney. After the bend to the left the track straightens out again and in some 150 yards one encounters a triangular junction of minor ways. The base of the triangle is a mere grassy track. Ignore this and follow the 'made up' track to the left, arriving in a few yards to the apex of the junction. At this point leave the track by going straight ahead entering an area of woods and scrubland aptly (in view of the rising gradients hitherto on the route) known as High Wood. Almost immediately on entering the woodland the path splits. Here take the left hand fork which appears to be the most used of the two footpaths. The clear path (highlighted by arrows painted on trees) emerges into the open after some 600 yards by way of a stile.

Keeping the same line of direction, the path crosses a largish field and re-enters woodland and descends rapidly, soon emerging into a field, veering slightly to the left and picking up the line of a hedge which keep on your left. After rising and approaching some housing in front of you, the path veers slightly to the right and follows in the form of a delightful little green alley between house gardens to emerge into a residential byway. Here turn left and after a pace or two go sharp right along a similar enclosed alleyway emerging into another byway, where turn right for a few yards emerging into the secondary road that serves the hamlet of . . .

BINFIELD HEATH, a meeting place of roads at an altitude of some 300 feet above sea level. The locality lost its pub in recent times and the only sign of commerce nowadays is the post office and adjacent village stores. It is a 'half way point' on a reasonably good 'bus service which links Reading and Henley, and which continues beyond the latter to serve Thameside Marlow and High Wycombe. Binfield Heath is a peaceful spot almost untouched by modern developments. Such a pity that it lost its pub!

After emerging into the aforementioned secondary road, turn sharp left and pass the post office and store on your right, following the road ahead, signposted to Shiplake. You are very soon in . . .

SHIPLAKE ROW, a collection of dwellings astride the road, with at a road junction ahead a peculiar circular brick edifice which appears to be something of an obsolete covered well(?).

The road then passes a house named Shiplake Rise on your right and then after some yards descends into a tree-lined cutting. Do not enter the cutting but follow a footpath on the left which runs close to, parallel and high above the road. Eventually after the road has almost completed its descent, the path disports itself into the highway by way of a few steep steps. Across the road and a few yards along is . . .

THE WHITE HART, an inn that has retained its original character on the outside, but which has been comfortably modernised within. The renowned Brakspear's ales are served but absent, on the author's visit, was the brewery's mild ale which is reasonably prolific in this vicinity. An enormous 'chalk board' indicates a great variety of tasty delicacies. There is a separate blackboard entitled 'pud news' with an equal variety of puddings and sweets. There are also restaurant facilities and it is significant to note that on Sunday mornings, only a traditional 'roast' is served – but, so the notice board states, a vegetarian alternative is also available – other pubs, please note!

Leave The White Hart and continue along the road, ignoring a fork on the left, to join in some half a mile the main Henley–Reading road which was encountered on the outward route, (at this crossroads is The Plowden Arms). Cross this main artery and proceed ahead along tiny Church Lane. Passing Shiplake parish church on your left, the way forward is via a sunken track which descends, punctuated by steps which were obviously installed to prevent the track becoming a watercourse after heavy rain. After the descent is completed you cross a concrete bridge over a small backwater. Having crossed this bridge, immediately turn sharp left across the top of a meadow, joining after some 100 yards The Thames Path which hugs the river from East London all the way to The Cotswolds. Follow this path for almost a mile, emerging then into a little road which leads to Shiplake Lock which is on your right. At the appropriate season you will be able to obtain teas and light refreshments at this venue. Having joined the lane go for a few paces to your right and then turn left along a path which crosses a meadows accompanied by the remains of a hedgerow. This clear path eventually takes a turn half left and emerges into a quiet byroad, where turn left immediately crossing another leafy backwater. At the road junction here go right (ignore the turning ahead which rises uphill). The way that you are in passes residential properties and emerges at the crossroads by The Corner Shop and The Baskerville Arms, where go right to return to Shiplake Station.

The author waiting for the train – Shiplake.

Walk 13

ISLIP to 'the Crown', CHARLTON-ON-OTMOOR and back

BY RAIL . . . Frequent service from London (Paddington) to Oxford, via Slough and Reading. Connecting service at 2 hourly intervals from Oxford to Islip on weekdays only. No Sunday service.

BY ROAD . . . From London area via Western Avenue on to M40 to junction 8, thence A40 (towards Oxford) for 2½ miles, turning right on to B4027 to Islip village. From points north of the London districts make for A41 and join at Hemel Hempstead, Berkhamsted, or Aylesbury, etc. From Aylesbury, take A418 through Thame to meet junction 8 of M40, thence as from London (see above).

MAP . . . Ordnance Survey Landranger Sheet 164.

DISTANCE OF WALK . . . Approximately 7½ miles.

TOPOGRAPHY . . . Almost equidistant from the Chiltern Escarpment and the dip slop of The Cotswolds lies the peculiar tract of flat land, Otmoor. The moor is now cultivated but in the not too distant past it resembled a wet fen. The walk does not encounter any gradients except shortly after the start a gentle rise to Noke village followed by a gentle descent to the levels of Otmoor. The country is by no means featureless, and has the character of extreme remoteness, despite its proximity to the City of Oxford. Except after a dry spell, the underfoot conditions can be rightly described a 'wet and puddly'.

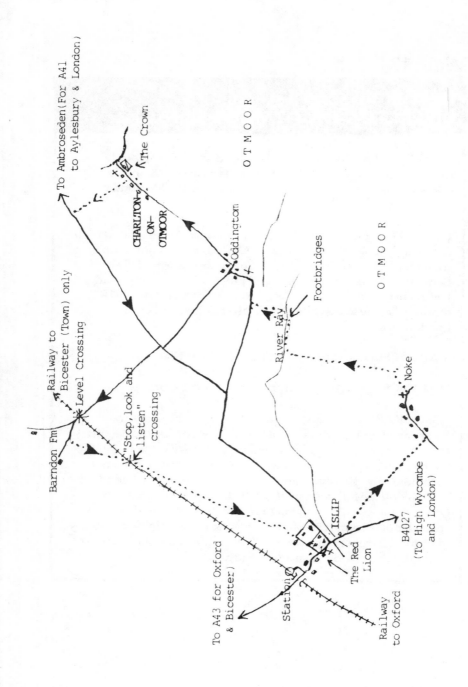

ISLIP STATION is a real gem of a country halt. It was closed to passengers for well over a quarter of a century and has now been rebuilt in the form of a short platform traversed by a single track with a plentitude of grass growing between the metals. In years to come the line may be upgraded to accommodate high speed trains from East Anglia to the West Country. If this project comes to pass, the really rural character will have disappeared for evermore!

A country station – Islip.

Leaving the station via the approach road, turn to your left on reaching the main B4027 road and follow this right through the attractive village of . . .

ISLIP, where the colour of many of the buildings indicate that one is not all that far away from 'Cotswold Oxfordshire'. There is a general shop and an attractive inn that proclaims outside that anything from snacks to steaks can be supplied. The village lays just north of the River Ray which is a tributary of the Cherwell, which is turn is a tributary of the Isis, the latter joining the River Thame at Oxfordshire's Dorchester, therefrom being the mighty Thames proper.

Having passed right through the village the road dips down to cross the Ray, which at this point flows ponderously, having gained little momentum after passing through the flats of Otmoor. After crossing the bridge the road rises quite sharply. Nearing the top of the rise, turn left on to a concreted drive, the signpost indicating that this is a part of the Oxfordshire Way. After some 20 yards fork right and thereafter follow the straight line of the clear path over several stiles rising gradually to surmount a low ridge of hills. The path then descends, becoming enclosed between hedges and winds its way downhill to emerge into a minor road at the approach to . . .

NOKE a spread out hamlet which has the attribute of lying at the end of a 'No Through Road'. (Surprising how many villages in this neighbourhood have the same characteristic.) There used to be a pub hereabouts, but alas it is no more. A peaceful place in which to dwell within some six miles from the teeming centre of Oxford City.

As you emerge from the path turn left and follow the road through the village, passing the parish church, St. Giles, on your left. The road then takes a right hand bend. Here go ahead on to a signposted bridleway which takes the form of a delightful 'green

St. Giles Church, Noke.

way'. After a few hundred yards you emerge at a T-junction of tracks, here turn left on to another green way which may be either overgrown and/or slightly waterlogged underfoot. You soon pass an iron gate and emerge upon a gravelly track. The way lies ahead and slightly right. The right of way herefrom is just outside the right hand hedge of the track. (There would not appear to by any infringement if you followed the track itself.) On your right lies the flat expanse of ...

OTMOOR, which is agricultural land now but which until drainage took place in the last century had the character of a wet sedge fen. the drainage was effected by the creation of a number of deep ditches and the re-routing of the river, hence around the north end of the moor the term, New River Ray, is now used to describe the main watercourse. Across the middle of Otmoor in a north–south direction lies the course of a Roman Road. Parts of the moor in the direction of the village of Horton-cum-Studley are used by the military – hence the signs on Ordnance Survey Maps, 'danger area'.

Gateway to Otmoor ... Footbridge over the River Ray.

After just in excess of a quarter of a mile the track veers off to the right to a silo. Ignore the direction towards the silo and continue ahead with the hedge of a large field on your right and so onwards dropping slightly downhill soon to be confronted by a deep drainage channel with nothing but a cattle ford ahead. Turn sharp right here and following the channel for some 300 yards, you come on your left to a handsome and modern wooden footbridge which not only crosses the drainage channel but also the lethargic course of the River Ray itself. Having crossed the bridges the path follows the right hand edge of a smallish field, emerging after some 75 yards to a junction of ways with a modern farmhouse to your right. Again the route lies ahead passing the farm buildings to your right, the path soon emerging at a farm drive which is in the form of an avenue of trees. You then emerge into a tiny road where turn right. In a short quarter of a mile after an attractive view across a meadow to the church, you enter the quiet village of . . .

ODDINGTON, an isolated place at the intersection of two very minor roads. As is so often the case the church seems to 'out-proportion' the village itself. It has been said that in bygone days

Oddington church.

a lantern was lit at the top of the tower to guide travellers home across the wastelands of Otmoor.

At the intersection of roads, keep a straight course as signposted to Charlton-on-Otmoor. In some three-quarters of a mile (you will have observed the church tower ahead) you are in the centre of . . .

CHARLTON-ON-OTMOOR. One of seven localities set around the perimeter of the moor and by far the largest. Apart from the garage of a coach operator, the village shows no signs of 'modern times'. The church tower looks down from its heights on to the main street, which is augmented with 'byways' on its northern side.

Towards the end of the village and on your right is . . .

THE CROWN, a really rural pub whose 'main line' so far as cask ales is concerned is the delicious Oxford Bitter from Morrells brewery in the City of Oxford. Pity that the pub does not do meals, but the friendly innkeeper explained that an enormous capital outlay would be needed if he took up catering. Potato crisps and nuts, etc. augment

the drinks, or if you feel so inclined a few rounds of sandwiches prepared before you leave home make pleasant eating in the fields encountered on the return route. Let not the absence of catering detract you from visiting The Crown – it really is a delightful and friendly place to linger over a drink or two.

Leaving The Crown, retrace your steps along the main street for a short way and look for a little alley on your right with the peculiar name of The Chure. Follow this between houses and on in a forward direction across a stile. The path crosses two fields with the hedge on your right and emerges into a secondary road, where turn right. Follow this quietish road from some three-quarters of a mile ignoring a 'no through road' turning on your right. At the next intersection of roads take the right hand turn, which like its predecessor is also dubbed with the same warning that it leads to nowhere in particular. Unlike the road to Noke encountered on the outward journey, this 'blind lane' leads not to a village but to a couple of isolated farms.

The tiny road eventually crosses the single track railway at a level crossing, after which take the left hand turning where the lane diverges. In a short way and some 200 yards before you reach the buildings of Barndon Farm, go to your left through a substantial gap in the hedge (no stile or gate here) and follow the track with the hedge on your left. After some 200 yards there is another substantial gap on your left. Go through this and resume your previous direction, this time with the hedge on your right. At the far right hand corner of this field cross a stile and a rather dilapidated plank bridge into a cluster of trees. After 50 yards the path rises to cross the railway line again by a 'stop, look and listen' signboard. The path crosses the railway on the skew and descends into a field, which cross keeping the same direction, gradually moving away from the railway embankment.

Crossing another stile and footbridge the line of the footpath hardly varies (the church tower of Islip can be seen ahead if visibility permits is a good directional landmark). Once again the next field is entered by way of a stile and little footbridge. The path keeps its course again, passing an isolated tree some 20 yards to your left and so onwards into the far left hand corner of the field. Here go through a gap by the gate and cross a more substantial brook by way of a 'railway sleeper' bridge. Immediately after the bridge turn left over a stile and follow the clear path which soon emerges via another stile into a road. Here go ahead, slightly rising to join the outward route in the centre of Islip village almost opposite the Red Lion. Turn right through the village and right into the station approach before the road crosses the railway.

Walk14

HANBOROUGH STATION to 'the Oxfordshire Yeoman', FREELAND, and back

BY RAIL . . . From London Paddington via Ealing, Slough, Reading and Oxford, etc. In other direction from Worcester and Moreton-in-Marsh, etc. Mainly hourly service, 2 hourly on Sundays.

BY ROAD . . . From London area via A40, M40 (to junction 8) then back on A40 to intersection with A44 where turn right. After 5 miles turn left on to A4095 (towards Witney). After 2 miles look for sign on left to Hanborough Station. From a more northerly direction aim for Aylesbury (see route for Walk 13). Thence A418 to A40 at Wheatley passing on route through Thame.

MAP . . . Ordnance Survey Sheet 164.

DISTANCE OF WALK . . . Approximately 6 miles.

TOPOGRAPHY . . . By Hanborough station the little River Evenlode pursues its way from deepest Cotswold country on route to The Isis (Thames). A few miles west of the City of Oxford you are virtually on the 'dip' slope of The Cotswolds. Grey stone walls and houses of similar hue give the rambler a sense of being close to the 'West Country'. This part of the county is well wooded, and with this in mind, regard with admiration the lovely vista of the river valley during the second half mile of the ramble. The route is slightly hilly but nothing in the way of a serious climb confronts the reader. As is the case with so many walks, stout footwear is recommended, except after dry warm spells. This is the most westerly ramble in the volume, and lovely to traverse at any season.

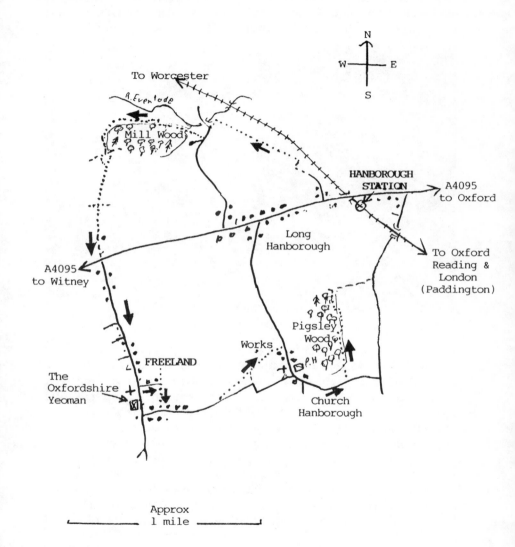

To Worcester

R. Evenlode

Mill Wood

HANBOROUGH STATION

A4095 to Oxford

A4095 to Witney

Long Hanborough

To Oxford Reading & London (Paddington)

Pigsley Wood

Works

P.H

FREELAND

The Oxfordshire Yeoman

Church Hanborough

Approx 1 mile

HANBOROUGH STATION is a distance of some three-quarters of a mile from Long Hanborough village. Adjacent to the railway is a 'bus museum with omnibuses of all shapes and colours within. The area around the station is in the valley of the River Evenlode, beyond which stream lie the extensive grounds of Blenheim Palace.

The River Evenlode.

Leave the single platform station and go along the narrow approach road to join the main A4095 road, where turn left. (The stone wall on the right hand side of the road reminds you that you are nearing Cotswold country.) Follow this road for a good half mile rising gently out of the valley. Just before entering the village street of Long Hanborough, turn right along a minor road, Park Lane. The sign at the entrance to the lane indicates 'no through road', a welcome sign when you are rambling. After passing pretty homesteads, the lane peters out and for a little way you traverse a green way shrouded with trees. Emerging from this the way ahead is via a clear path with the hedge on your right. You are descending here into the Evenlode Valley. Soon the path changes its mind and crosses to the other side of the hedge and proceeds forward to eventually join a rough track which comes in from your right. Turn to your left here (a pretty stretch of the Evenlode is now on your immediate right). On joining a metalled byroad, continue ahead from some 100 yards to a point where there is a mineral water depot on your right.

Just to the right of the spa water premises is a stile. Cross this and follow a clear path which soon enters wooded ground, with a steep hillside on your left. Be careful not to slip sideways hereabouts – the camber in places is acute! Without turning right or left you eventually come to a spot where with a right hand turn and then a left the way resuming its course now just outside the woodland. Veering round leftwards the path ascends quite sharply and eventually joins a rough track where bear left soon scaling the top of the rising ground. You then come to a junction of tracks. Here turn right just for a pace or two and then sharp left along another clear path with the hedge on your left. In some 20 yards you meet another pathway. bear right and follow this for a good half mile. The path then becomes a track in the neighbourhood of a dwelling and a little further on disports itself back into the main A4095 at a

Victorian Baroque church – Freeland.

T-junction. Cross the main road to the turning opposite, Wroslyn Road as signposted to Freeland. In about three-quarters of a mile you reach to old village centre of . . .

FREELAND, a 'strung out' sort of village (as you may have noticed on your traverse of Wroslyn Road) with the best to come at the end. Its infrequent omnibus services and its lack of proximity to a railway station obviously makes it a suitable dormitory for Oxford commuters with their own private transport.

Passing the Victorian Baroque parish church and rounding a slight bend, you suddenly encounter upon your right . . .

THE OXFORDSHIRE YEOMAN, this pleasantly fronted building has before it a large south facing beer garden and accommodation within is just as roomy. Local (Morrells) beer from the City of Oxford is amongst the refreshment served and choices of food are abundant and reasonably priced.

Leaving the pub, retrace your footsteps, crossing the road. In a short way, take a turning to your right called Blenheim Lane (like Park Lane in Hanborough, adorned with a 'no through road' sign).

The lane soon ends with a footpath going to the right and left. Take the right hand branch going over a stile and passing along the left hand margin of a recreation field. Emerging in the left hand corner of this field, via another stile you turn left into a bylane which soon leaves the outposts of the village behind. The narrow lane then descends and on the descent look for a path on your left. Crossing the entry stile the path descends to a valley just to the right of a water treatment works. Crossing the approach drive to these works and a tiny 'babbling brook' (you can always hear it but it is much of the year hidden in undergrowth), ascend sharply in the next field, gradually moving away from the hedge on your left and aiming somewhat diagonally towards a high coniferous boundary of a house. Hidden in the boundary is a gap which leads into a tiny enclosed path which soon leads out into a secondary road. Here turn right and traverse the village of . . .

CHURCH HANBOROUGH, a classical English village set on high ground between little valleys. You will have noted the magnificent spire of the church on your approach. On your left is the lovely old inn, The Hand and Shears, and the grey stone of the buildings reminds you once more that you are on the verge of The Cotswold Hills.

Leaving the village behind the road begins to descend gradually and on coming to a slight right hand bend and just before some farm outbuildings on your left, turn left along a footpath which runs along the right hand side of a field, then entering woodlands (Pigsley Wood). The path starts by running just inside the trees and then just outside. You then come to a waymark which indicated that the right of way goes rightwards and diagonally across an open field. Here go back into the woods and follow a fairly well used way which keeps more or less just inside the wood. Eventually you come to a crossing track, where turn right to leave Pigsley Wood. (There is hereabouts a sign indicating an official diversion of the right of way, hence the well trodden way that you have enjoyed.)

The ensuing track follows a hedge on its left and soon emerges into a road. Here turn left and having gone under a railway bridge this road leads on to join the main A4095, where turn left again and proceed for some third of a mile to the narrow lane that forms the approach to Hanborough station.

INDEX

W = Walk Number

A companion volume to this book covers

PUB WALKS
from
COUNTRY STATIONS
in
Bedfordshire and Hertfordshire

* * *

The Book Castle also publishes a variety of walks books by Nick Moon with a wide range of rambles in Buckinghamshire and Oxfordshire – over 150 across his three different series. See the following pages for details. Available via all bookshops.

* * *

Books Published by
THE BOOK CASTLE

COUNTRYSIDE CYCLING IN BEDFORDSHIRE,
BUCKINGHAMSHIRE AND HERTFORDSHIRE: Mick Payne.
Twenty rides on- and off-road for all the family.

PUB WALKS FROM COUNTRY STATIONS:
Bedfordshire and Hertfordshire: Clive Higgs.
Fourteen circular country rambles, each starting and finishing at a
railway station and incorporating a pub-stop at a mid-way point.

PUB WALKS FROM COUNTRY STATIONS:
Buckinghamshire and Oxfordshire: Clive Higgs.
A further selection of unusual rural rambles.

LOCAL WALKS: South Bedfordshire and North Chilterns:
Vaughan Basham.
Twenty-seven thematic circular walks.

LOCAL WALKS: North and Mid Bedfordshire: Vaughan Basham.
Twenty-five thematic circular walks.

FAMILY WALKS: Chilterns South: Nick Moon.
Thirty 3 to 5 mile circular walks.

FAMILY WALKS: Chilterns North: Nick Moon.
Thirty further shortish country walks.

CHILTERN WALKS: Hertfordshire, Bedfordshire and
North Buckinghamshire: Nick Moon.
CHILTERN WALKS: Buckinghamshire: Nick Moon.
CHILTERN WALKS: Oxfordshire and West Buckinghamshire:
Nick Moon.
A trilogy of circular walks, in association with the Chiltern Society.
Each volume contains 30 circular walks.

OXFORDSHIRE WALKS:
Oxford, the Cotswolds and the Cherwell Valley: Nick Moon.
OXFORDSHIRE WALKS:
Oxford, the Downs and the Thames Valley: Nick Moon.
Two volumes that complement Chiltern Walks: Oxfordshire and
complete coverage of the county, in association with the Oxford
Fieldpaths Society. Thirty circular walks in each.

JOURNEYS INTO BEDFORDSHIRE: Anthony Mackay.
Foreword by The Marquess of Tavistock, Woburn Abbey. A lavish book of over 150 evocative ink drawings.

MANORS and MAYHEM, PAUPERS and PARSONS: Tales from Four Shire: Beds., Bucks., Herts., and Northants.: John Houghton
Little-known historical snippets and stories.

MYTHS and WITCHES, PEOPLE and POLITICS: Tales from Four Shires: Bucks., Beds., Herts., and Northants.: John Houghton.
Anthology of strange, but true historical events.

HISTORIC FIGURES IN THE BUCKINGHAMSHIRE LANDSCAPE: John Houghton.
Major personalities and events that have shaped the county's past, including a special section on Bletchley Park.

FOLK: Characters and Events in the History of Bedfordshire and Northamptonshire: Vivienne Evans.
Anthology about people of yesteryear – arranged alphabetically by village or town.

BEDFORDSHIRE'S YESTERYEARS Vol 2:
The Rural Scene: Brenda Fraser Newstead.
Vivid first-hand accounts of country life two or three generations ago.

BEDFORDSHIRE'S YESTERYEARS Vol 3:
Craftsmen and Tradespeople: Brenda Fraser Newstead.
Fascinating recollections over several generations practising many vanishing crafts and trades.

BEDFORDSHIRE'S YESTERYEARS Vol 4:
Wat Times and Civil Matters: Brenda Fraser Newstead.
Two World Wars, plus transport, law and order, etc.

THE RAILWAY AGE IN BEDFORDSHIRE: Fred Cockman.
Classic, illustrated account of early railway history.

GLEANINGS REVISITED:
Nostalgic Thoughts of a Bedfordshire Farmer's Boy:
E W O'Dell.
His own sketches and early photographs adorn this lively account of rural Bedfordshire in days gone by.

FARM OF MY CHILDHOOD, 1925–1947: Mary Roberts.
An almost vanished lifestyle on a remote farm near Flitwick.

SWANS IN MY KITCHEN: Lis Dorer.
Story of a Swan Sanctuary near Hemel Hempstead.

DUNSTABLE WITH THE PRIORY: 1100–1550: Vivienne Evans.
Dramatic growth of Henry I's important new town around a major crossroads.

DUNSTABLE DECADE: THE EIGHTIES:
A Collection of Photographs: Pat Lovering.
A souvenir book of 300 pictures of people and events in the 1980s.

DUNSTABLE IN DETAIL: Nigel Benson.
A hundred of the town's buildings and features, plus town trail map.

OLD DUNSTABLE: Bill Twaddle.
A new edition of this collection of early photographs.

BOURNE and BRED: A Dunstable Boyhood Between the Wars:
Colin Bourne.
An elegantly written, well-illustrated book capturing the spirit of the town over fifty years ago.

ROYAL HOUGHTON: Pat Lovering:
Illustrated history of Houghton Regis from the earliest times to the present.

THE CHANGING FACE OF LUTON: An Illustrated History:
Stephen Bunker, Robin Holgate and Marian Nichols.
Luton's development from earliest times to the present busy industrial town. Illustrated in colour and monochrome

THE MEN WHO WORE STRAW HELMETS:
Policing Luton, 1840–1974: Tom Madigan.
Meticulously chronicled history; dozens of rare photographs; author served in Luton Police for fifty years.

BETWEEN THE HILLS: The Story of Lilley, a Chiltern Village:
Roy Pinnock.
A priceless piece of our heritage – the rural beauty remains but the customs and way of life described here have largely disappeared.

A HATTER GOES MAD!: Kristina Howells.
Luton Town footballers, officials and supporters talk to a female fan.

LEGACIES: Tales and Legends of Luton and the North Chilterns:
Vic Lea.
Twenty-five mysteries and stories based on fact, including Luton Town Football Club. Many photographs.

LEAFING THROUGH LITERATURE:
Writers' Lives in Hertfordshire and Bedfordshire: David Carroll.
Illustrated short biographies of many famous authors and their connections with these counties.

A PILGRIMAGE IN HERTFORDSHIRE: H M Alderman.
Classic, between-the-wars tour round the county, embellished with line drawings.

CHILTERN ARCHAEOLOGY: RECENT WORK:
A Handbook for the Next Decade: edited by Robin Holgate.
The latest views, results and excavations by twenty-three leading archaeologists throughout the Chilterns.

THE HILL OF THE MARTYR:
An Architectural History of St. Albans Abbey: Eileen Roberts.
Scholarly and readable chronological narrative history of Hertfordshire and Bedfordshire's famous cathedral. Fully illustrated with photographs and plans.

THE TALL HITCHIN SERGEANT:
A Victorian Crime Novel Based on Fact: Edgar Newman.
Mixes real police officers and authentic background with an exciting storyline.

THE TALL HITCHIN INSPECTOR'S CASEBOOK:
A Victorian Crime Novel Based on Fact: Edgar Newman.
Worthies of the time encounter more archetypal villains.

SPECIALLY FOR CHILDREN

VILLA BELOW THE KNOLLS: A Story of Roman Britain:
Michael Dundrow.
An exciting adventure for young John in Totternhoe and Dunstable two thousand years ago.

THE RAVENS: One Boy Against the Might of Rome:
James Dyer.
On the Barton Hills and in the south-east of England as the men of the great fort of Ravensburgh (near Hexton) confront the invaders.

Further titles are in preparation.
All the above are available via any bookshop, or from the publisher and bookseller

THE BOOK CASTLE
12 Church Street, Dunstable Bedfordshire, LU5 4RU
Tel: (01582) 605670